A SOCIAL MARKET IN HOUSING

Tom Startup

with supplementary material by
Jim Kemeny and Philippe Thalmann

THE SOCIAL MARKET FOUNDATION

The Foundation's main activity is to commission and publish original papers by independent academic and other experts on key topics in the economic and social fields, with a view to stimulating public discussion on the performance of markets and the social framework within which they operate.

The Foundation is a registered charity and a company limited by guarantee. It is independent of any political party or group and is financed by the sales of publications and by voluntary donations from individuals, organisations and companies.

The views expressed in publications are those of the authors and do not represent a corporate opinion of the Foundation.

Acknowledgments

I would like to thank the staff of the Social Market Foundation for continuing support for my work in this area. In particular, thanks are due to Philip Collins, for patient re-readings and important words of encouragement.

In terms of specific intellectual content, I owe a great deal to Professor Jim Kemeny whose ideas inspired me to write this in the first place and whose continuing support and encouragement through the admittedly unsatisfactory medium of email was vital.

Particular thanks go to the following people who kindly read an earlier draft and provided helpful comments and criticisms: Brian Pomeroy, Professor Philippe Thalmann, and Ian Fletcher.

First published by The Social Market Foundation, June 2003

The Social Market Foundation
11 Tufton Street
London, SW1P 3QB

Contents

Executive Summary

This paper argues that there are serious structural problems with the provision of housing in the UK. The main problems are:

- Inadequate levels of house-building and investment which result from a burdensome and inappropriate planning system, poor incentives to expand supply and government interference. This has caused medium to long-term affordability problems.

- Problems associated with mass home-ownership: macroeconomic instability, labour market immobility and financial risk to low income households.

- A distorted and bizarre relationship between the three main tenures which artificially pushes people into either social housing or home-ownership.

Government reforms set out in *The Sustainable Communities Plan*, *The Planning and Compulsory Purchase Bill* and the draft *Housing Bill* won't work because:

- There is no fundamental reform of the planning system. It will remain a slow, cumbersome and 'plan-led' system which will have the effect of keeping levels of new build at artificially low levels. Indeed the government has increased the restrictions imposed on private development through the use of minimum densities and requirements for affordable housing.

- The level of public funding committed to expanding supply is insufficient to bring about the required 'step-change' in supply.

- The government has no real commitment to changing the fundamental relationship between home-ownership, private renting and social housing. Indeed it is persisting in artificially encouraging low income households to become home-owners - a commitment which is hard for those households to maintain when economic conditions deteriorate.

This paper argues that structural reform of the provision of housing is necessary if we are to ensure the appropriate levels of new building and affordable housing for all. The main elements of this 'social market in housing' are:

- A liberalised planning regime

- No direct state provision of housing

- A fiscal and regulatory structure which is broadly neutral between Registered Social Landlords (RSLs), private renting and home-ownership

- Housing benefit entitlement based on household size, income and local costs but not actual housing costs.

To this end, the specific policy proposals outlined in this paper are:

Priority 1: Promoting an Expansion of New Building

- Introduce land value taxation on unused / unproductive land held by developers.

- Abolish the 'plan-led' system of managing housing supply in favour of using the planning system to specify (only) which areas cannot be used for housing, with the implication that all other areas can be used for housing.

- Abolish requirements for minimum densities, proportions of affordable housing and attributes of 'sustainability'. Only use 106 agreements to provide for necessary local infrastructure.

Priority 2: Improving Provision for Low Income Households

- Set a deadline for the transfer of council housing to RSLs (18-24 months). No new tenancies should be awarded. As homes become vacant they should be sold on to an RSL.

- Ensure that no RSL has an unreasonable local monopoly on cost renting by requiring transfers to occur to more than one RSL.

- Phase-out all capital subsidies to RSLs and councils.

- Gradual deregulation of RSLs but allow tax exemption for charitable status.

- Housing Benefit Reform: a generous income subsidy, related to household size and local costs, but not actual housing costs. Could eventually be assimilated into general income support.

- Consider setting a housing benefit premium payable to providers of housing for those households in receipt of Housing Benefit.

Priority 3: Reducing Tenure Bias

- Introduce (phase-in) 40% Capital Gains Tax on home-owners.

- Introduce an annual property tax on home-owners (based on a proportion of the imputed rental income or market value of the property) - say 1.5% of the market value of the property - with deductions permitted for maintenance costs and interest on debt.

- Abolish council tax.

- Abolish stamp duty on all housing transactions.

- Abolish government-subsidised home-ownership schemes, such as The Starter Home Initiative.

- Over time, seek to harmonise the treatment of private landlords and RSLs making them both subject to roughly the same fiscal and regulatory system.

Introduction

In recent years housing has not been seen as a major priority for the government, compared to say the standard of education in schools or care provided by the National Health Service. This is for a variety of reasons. One reason is that the vast majority of people have a satisfactory home to live in, and so, by and large, they do not have substantial complaints to make about housing policy. Another reason is that, unlike health and education, the state is not the major provider of housing in the UK. Only 15% of households still live in directly state provided housing[1], although considerably more rely on the state to finance their housing. So, rightly or wrongly, housing problems are often not seen as the direct responsibility of government. Finally, many perceived problems in housing are properly seen as problems that really lie in a different policy area. For instance, the problem of homelessness is seen by many as being mainly the result of a complex set of forces, including poverty, alcohol and drug abuse, unemployment and the breakdown of families; it is not really a problem to do with housing *per se*.[2]

Against this complacency I would suggest that one reason for taking housing seriously is that we spend an awful lot of public money on it. We spend around £5 billion of public money on housing every year, and a further £12 billion on housing benefit[3], bringing the total public expenditure to at least £17 billion a year. This may seem relatively small compared with the £72 billion on health and £51 billion on education spent each year.[4] But we must remember that whereas health and education are comprehensive services available to all (and so the average private expenditure of households on health and education is very small), only 20% of households are housed by councils or Registered Social Landlords[5], with around one in six households in receipt of housing benefit. So we spend

---

[1] Wilcox, S. (2003). *UK Housing Review 2002/2003*. Joseph Rowntree Foundation. Table 17d, p. 91.
[2] This approach is related to the development and importance of the concept of 'social exclusion' – a term used to refer to the coincidence of a cluster of related problems. See e.g. the work of the Social Exclusion Unit.
[3] Quantified as Total Managed Expenditure. Treasury figures.
[4] Wilcox, op. cit, table 15a, p. 83.
[5] Source: ODPM.

around £17 billion on housing each year and yet that public money is probably spent on no more than one in four households – the rest of us having to provide for ourselves in the market place. So given the expense it is worth asking if it is money spent well.

Another reason for taking it seriously is that it is one class of goods which can reasonably be called a 'necessity' – something more or less everyone places great value on. It is therefore essential that we get the provision of housing right. As I hope to show in Chapter 1, there are serious deficiencies in the provision of housing which could valuably be remedied. Last there is the thought that the short-term neglect of housing may be politically acceptable at the moment, but it will come back to haunt future governments.[6]

It is worth saying a few more things about why this report has been written. First, as I say above, this is not intended as an academic exercise. It is written by someone who believes that there are serious structural flaws in the housing market which could valuably be remedied. The flaws and the means of remedying them are the primary subject of this paper.

Second, while there is much good policy work being done at the moment in government, academia and think tanks, there seems to me a lack of any strategic vision of what the housing market, as a whole, ought to look like. This is unsatisfactory for two reasons. First, the housing market is complicated, and there are important and powerful interactions between different sectors, and therefore different policy areas. So it is misleading merely to focus on the problems in say, social housing, without also looking at the relationship between social housing and home-ownership, or to look at housing benefit, without also looking at how rents are determined in both social and privately rented accommodation. So, perhaps more so than in other areas of policy, an overview of the entire provision of housing is required if policy is to be properly integrated into a coherent programme of reform.

This piece attempts to outline both a general approach to housing policy and an overview of what the sector should look like.

---

[6] Walker, D. (2002, March 6). Home Truths. *The Guardian.*

Chapter 1 sets out the main problems with the provision of housing in the UK which are: the very low levels of new building and investment, various problems associated with mass-home-ownership, and the unfair and inefficient treatment of private renting relative to home-ownership and social housing.

In Chapter 2 I discuss the main recent government policy initiatives set out in *The Planning and Compulsory Purchase Bill, The Sustainable Communities Plan* and the draft *Housing Bill*. I argue that the reforms won't succeed in addressing any of the main problems and may even make things worse because they are not radical enough and do not provide the structural reform needed.

In Chapter 3 I present a radical alternative model for housing provision entitled "A Social Market in Housing". It is a 'social market' because it attempts to make extensive use of market forces, while endeavouring to ensure that social ends – in particular a desire to ensure that everyone has access to a decent standard of accommodation – are fulfilled. The main elements of this model are:

- No direct state provision of housing
- A liberalised planning regime
- A fiscal and regulatory structure which is broadly neutral between RSLs, private renting and home-ownership
- Housing benefit entitlement based on household size, income and local costs but not actual housing costs.

In Chapter 4 I set out the main policy changes that would be necessary to bring about a transition from the current system to the social market model.

The Appendix includes two pieces which explain and elaborate variants on the social market approach. Professor Jim Kemeny presents an overview of developments in Sweden. Professor Philippe Thalmann provides an overview of the Swiss model. Their contributions show, in a number of ways, how other European countries have pursued models which exhibit much greater neutrality between tenures and consequently have rental sectors which enjoy widespread popularity.

Chapter 1

Housing in the UK: Persistent Problems

In this chapter I will argue that there are serious and persistent problems in the structure of housing provision in the UK. Levels of new building and investment are too low, mass home-ownership has a number of serious drawbacks, and the relationship between the three main tenures – home-ownership, private renting and social housing - is unfair and fosters serious inefficiencies. All this means that the very high levels of public expenditure on housing are being badly wasted.

Low Levels of Building and Investment

One striking problem with the current state of housing in the UK is the very low levels of house-building, now at their lowest levels since statistics began[7]. This is despite what were, until recently, booming house prices in most areas. Indeed Britain has invested very little in its housing stock over the past 20 years. Only around 18% of Gross Capital Formation has been spent on housing over the past twenty years, compared to typical levels of around 20-30% among other European nations.[8] Furthermore, the size of dwellings in the UK is low and, extraordinarily, falling – a trend not found in any other EU nation.[9] The UK also has a very small number of dwellings for its population and a housing stock which is comparatively old.[10] The only positive note is that most housing is relatively well-equipped, with nearly all dwellings having a bath/shower and 88% having central heating. The picture that emerges is of British people living in houses which are smaller and older than those inhabited by their European neighbours.[11] Quite simply, while in many cases we have become a much wealthier nation over the past few decades and standards of living have improved dramatically,

---

[7] See official ODPM statistics dating back to 1949.
[8] European Union (2001), *Housing Statistics in the European Union 2001*. Table 1.13, p. 18.
[9] Ibid. Table 2.1, p. 24.
[10] Ibid. p. 27
[11] Incidentally we live in smaller properties than countries which have comparable or higher population density, e.g. the Netherlands and Belgium.

we are not living in much bigger or better accommodation than we were a generation ago.

Low levels of house-building are also a problem because, over time, they have a direct impact on the affordability of housing. They also contribute to problems of over-crowding and homelessness. With new additions having only a marginal effect on the overall supply of housing, fluctuations in demand, if not met by a steady increase in supply, will have a serious impact on prices. This will generate affordability problems for both potential buyers and tenants in the private rental sector. Average house prices in London are around 4.8 times the average salary, compared with a long-term trend of 3.3.[12] This means that buying is increasingly difficult to afford for households with modest incomes, particularly first time buyers.[13]

So why are levels of building so low? There are a number of reasons for this. Firstly, local authorities have more or less ceased building because they are not given central government support to pay for it. Housing associations, which do receive state support for new build through the Housing Corporation, have expanded their own building levels, but not nearly enough to maintain the levels historically achieved by local authorities. Meanwhile, private builders have continued to build at around the same level for about 10 years – between 150,000 and 200,000 a year.

But why have housing associations and private developers not expanded their output to meet the obvious demand? This is a difficult question. One frequently cited factor is the planning system. House-builders typically complain that the planning system is too slow and inefficient, the result being that levels of new building are kept artificially low due to the slow progress of planning application. The government tended to agree with this analysis in its original Green Paper and was, if anything, even more disparaging.[14] There the planning system was described as "inflexible, legalistic and bureaucratic".[15] Development was being "blocked" rather than

---

[12] Figures from Nationwide Building Society, and Cambridge Econometrics. Figures relate to 2001.
[13] Recent falls in interest rates have largely served to preserve the affordability of housing, measured in relation to monthly outgoings. However, with correspondingly lower levels of inflation, affordability over the term of the mortgage has worsened.
[14] Department of the Environment Transport and the Regions (2001). *Planning: Delivering a Fundamental Change.*
[15] Ibid, Foreword by Stephen Byers

promoted.[16] The system was "complex, remote, hard to understand and difficult to access". Plans were often inconsistent. National planning guidance was "long and often unfocussed". The rules were "unclear". The appeals procedure seemed "obscure" to many people. The speed of decision-making was "slow and variable", with local authorities often failing to reach their target of making a decision within 8 weeks. Outcomes were uncertain, and the process of updating plans was slow and expensive. Appeals were dealt with too slowly. Overall, the planning system was obviously in need of a serious overhaul. The Green Paper contained a number of promising proposals, some of which have been retained in the forthcoming *Planning and Compulsory Purchase Bill* (discussed in the next chapter).

But not only is the planning system slow and inefficient, more importantly, it remains a 'plan-led system'. That is, the possibility of development still depends on the consistency or otherwise of proposed developments with the antecedently determined priorities of regional and national planning authorities. So it is still taken to be the job of government agencies to decide on the amount, type and location of future residential developments despite the fact that government agencies have ceased house-building themselves. And as the priorities of the government and private developers increasingly diverge this is a recipe for a planning system which obstructs rather than facilitates new building. Green Belts, which cover 12% of land in England, and constitute an enormous restriction on the location of new developments, are a case in point. Their existence is an enormous barrier to potential future developments.

A further crucial factor in the problem of low-supply is land. Housing associations who might want to build new houses often find that the land necessary to build is either unavailable (not for sale) or too expensive to make the investment affordable. Alternatively land may be held in the expectation of future increases in prices. Local authorities, or other public bodies, can often be the worst offenders in such cases, required by 'best value' to sell their land for the highest prices they can obtain.

In terms of private development unfortunately, the whole business is shrouded in mystery due to a lack of information about how much private developers hold and what proportion of it is eligible for residential

---

[16] Ibid.

development. What data there is shows us that developable land banks (i.e. land with planning permission) in the UK are small and decreasing. Only 15% of land held by developers is developable.[17] But the key question is: Has the rest of the land had planning permission denied (or perhaps delayed), or has planning permission merely not been requested? Unfortunately there is, as yet, no definitive way of answering this question. However, given that 90% of planning applications are eventually approved[18], the most plausible explanation seems to be that developers are not currently seeking planning permission for a large proportion of their land. The question is: why?

One plausible explanation is that developers are seeking to time their developments in order to maximise profits, and have been waiting on rising house prices. Another part of the explanation is that they are nervous about the state of the housing market, and don't wish to initiate large scale developments in case the market crashes and they face trying to sell new properties when prices are at their lowest. So the very volatility of the housing market acts as an important deterrent to developers. Another factor is that government planning restrictions may make developers feel that planning permission for housing is very unlikely to be granted. Importantly, developers, knowing that local authorities often face specific targets to reach in terms of new building, will be reluctant to reach those targets too quickly, which might mean that subsequent planning permissions would be hard to come by. Better, perhaps, to keep levels of new applications at lower levels but with greater certainty that they will be approved.

So the problem of under-supply is a complicated one, but the main factors are the government's aggressive use of a slow and inefficient planning system and the volatility of the housing market. The combination of these two factors tends to have the effect of keeping levels of new development artificially low.

---

[17] FPD Savills (2003, March), *UK Land & Development Research Bulletin.* p. 3
[18] DETR op. cit., section 1.7.

Problems of Mass Home-Ownership

A century of government policy has had the cumulative effect of pushing those who can afford to do so to buy their own home, with around 70% of households now home-owners. For many households, this has proved to be a beneficial development, providing them with an asset which has increased substantially in value. Home-ownership can often be a force for encouraging saving and provides a resource which households can fall back on in times of need. But mass home-ownership is a development which also has many serious disadvantages.

Mass home-ownership, particularly when it is largely financed through debt, tends to generate a very volatile boom and bust cycle in house prices. This volatility means that in boom times, the market leaves increasing numbers of people unable to afford to buy or rent desirable properties, and in times of slump thousands of people face negative equity or repossession. At the nadir of the crash in the early 1990s one in thirteen households was left in negative equity. There were also 75,540 repossessions in one year, and a further 275,000 in arrears of 6 months or more. In 2001, amid a booming housing market and stable economic conditions there were still 18,000 repossessions and a further 60,000 in mortgage arrears of 6 months or more.[19] The consequences when the next crash occurs could be very severe.

Home-ownership has also been extended very far down the income scale, making a large number of people very vulnerable to macroeconomic shocks, largely outside their control, which could undermine their ability to afford to make repayments. 15% of outright owners and a further 17% of those with a mortgage are classified as living in poverty.[20] According to the government's figures, around 21% of working-age people below the poverty line own their own home outright, with a further 28% owning their own home with a mortgage.[21] So, many of these low income home-owners therefore end up relying on some form of state support. Although falling, there are still 220,000 recipients of income support for mortgage interest,

---

[19] Wilcox op. cit. Table 49, p. 136
[20] Burrows, R. (2003). *Homeownership and Poverty in Britain.* Joseph Rowntree Foundation. NB the poverty measure used is not the government's official measure, but a level set on the basis of the non-possession of 'socially perceived necessities'.
[21] Department for Work and Pensions, (2002a), *Households Below Average Income 2000/1.*Chapter 5, table 5.6.

claiming an average level of assistance of £25 per week.[22] In total, 5% of home-owners with a mortgage and 11% of outright owners are in receipt of some form of income-based benefit.[23] Arguably, many households, particularly those with low and/or uncertain incomes, are ill-suited to home-ownership, or later become so. Plausibly many such households would be better off with the less demanding commitments associated with renting.

Mass home-ownership also generates significant problems for the economy more generally due to the relationship between house prices, consumer demand and the cost of business investment. In times of economic difficulties lower interest rates may be a useful tool for expanding business investment. However they also tend to boost demand for housing and lead to excessive consumer debt. A desire to 'cool' the housing market through raising or maintaining interest rates may conflict with a desire to stimulate business investment. In the past few months the Bank of England has consistently refused to lower interest rates (despite strong demands from the manufacturing sector) for fear of unleashing yet further rises in house prices.

Another problem associated with mass home-ownership concerns its relationship with unemployment. It has been shown by Andrew Oswald that high levels of home-ownership are very strongly correlated with levels of unemployment.[24] The explanation he offers for this is that home-ownership does not help foster a flexible labour market – an important condition for producing low levels of unemployment. Home-owners are less able to move to find alternative work should they face redundancy, particularly if they also experience negative equity. Conversely, when property values are increasing home-owners are less willing to move or seek more profitable employment, instead being able to benefit from equity withdrawal. Furthermore, Oswald finds that the proportion of private renters is strongly but *inversely* correlated with levels of unemployment in a country. That is, the more private renters it has, the less unemployment a country tends to

---

[22] Department for Work and Pensions (2002b, November), Income Support Quarterly Statistical Enquiry.
[23] Department for Work and Pensions (2003), *Family Resources Survey 2000-01*. Table 3.20, p.64.
[24] Oswald, A. (1999), "The Housing Market and Europe's Unemployment: A Non-Technical Paper", available at: http://www2.warwick.ac.uk/fac/soc/economics/staff/faculty/oswald/homesnt.pdf

have. So perhaps there are good reasons to favour a larger, more attractive rental market if we wish to improve labour mobility and employment levels.

The government has recently shown an awareness of the problem, citing a connection between the housing market, labour immobility and lower levels of productivity. It has acknowledged that labour mobility is poor in the UK partly because of the housing market with both home-owners and social housing tenants tending to be immobile relative to private renters. However, the main reason cited by the Treasury is the fact of great regional variations in house prices and prices-earnings ratios.[25]

This is related to a final and crucial point. Substantial house price inflation over the medium to long term, and across virtually all geographical areas (as we've seen in the UK for some years) can, in fact, only be maintained by an artificial restriction on supply. This is where the problems of mass home-ownership meet with the puzzle of very low building levels. Low building levels are a significant cause of general house price inflation which, in turn, continues to fuel the desire for home-ownership. This is because inflation in the value of one's home is one of the primary reasons for the attractiveness of home-ownership. Simply, this inflation is what reinforces the perception of home-ownership as a 'good investment'. In contrast, France and Germany have seen real house prices remain roughly constant over the past twenty years.[26] So there, home-ownership, as an investment, is a much less attractive proposition.

This is not to suggest that low levels of house-building are part of a 'conspiracy' to maintain house prices for home-owners. Rather, in an environment in which 70% of households are home-owners there is unlikely to be any substantial political gain in big house-building programmes which might lead to constant or falling house prices over the medium to long term. The political cost of the affordability problems for the small number of households trying to buy their first home, or renting privately, are likely to be substantially outweighed by the political costs of reducing house price inflation for existing home-owners.

---

[25]HM Treasury (2003). *The Budget 2003*, p. 72. However the analysis presented is not very convincing. Such ratios are also highly variable in comparable countries with much better labour mobility.

[26] The Economist (2002, November 16th). House Prices: British Exceptionalism.

The fact remains, however, that with inadequate levels of supply, affordability problems will emerge and worsen until building levels increase and house prices drop or remain static.

So, mass home-ownership in the UK causes macroeconomic instability, reduces labour mobility and generates significant financial risk for low-income households. Low levels of house-building are part of the case of house-price inflation and thereby contribute to the relative attractiveness to home-ownership as a tenure.

The Distorted Relationship Between Tenures

The history of housing in the UK has left us with very peculiar and unfair differences between types of tenure. Despite the recent abolition of Mortgage Interest Tax Relief, home-ownership still receives very preferential treatment under the tax system, being exempt from Capital Gains Tax. Council tax – what is often thought of as a 'property tax' – is really a tax on residence rather than property, and rates are only very roughly proportional to the market value of the property inhabited. The upshot is that UK home-owners benefit from one of the most generous fiscal environments in the western world. In contrast, Sweden imposes 25% VAT on new homes, a tax on imputed rental values and a capital gains tax on homeowners. Swiss home-owners face a tax on imputed rental values and must pay a capital gains tax but are eligible for interest relief.[27]

At the other end of the spectrum, council and housing association tenants receive substantial state subsidies indirectly in the form of capital grants and loans, and directly in the form of regulated rents, housing benefit and security for tenants. In addition many of these tenants have the right to buy their properties at a hefty discount.[28]

Within council housing, rents bear little relation to the size, quality, or attractiveness of a property, with two comparable properties often

---

[27] Balchin, P. (1996). *Housing Policy in Europe*, p. 30.
[28] The right to buy applies to all council tenants (with some exemptions) and all housing association tenants who were previously council tenants but transferred to a housing association under the Large Scale Voluntary Transfer Scheme.

attracting very different rents with no apparent explanation for the difference. The relationship between council tenants and housing association tenants is also peculiar, with the latter usually paying considerably higher rents than the former, even if there is no difference in the attractiveness of the property. This is partly due to the greater protections afforded to council tenants and the higher levels of indebtedness of housing associations.

In between home-owners and tenants of social housing are those who are in the private rental sector and receive very little in the way of state support or subsidy[29]. Private landlords are subject to relatively heavy taxation, having to pay Capital Gains Tax, with rental income treated as ordinary income and taxed accordingly[30]. Nor do they receive anything like the state grants and subsidised loans which housing associations receive. Private tenants typically have little security of tenure and rents are usually high – substantially higher than for tenants in comparable properties in either housing associations or council properties and often more expensive than the cost of servicing a mortgage on a comparable property. Average rents in 2000 for local authorities were £45, housing associations (assured), £54, and private rents (unfurnished), £77.[31]

This differential treatment is both unfair and inefficient. It is unfair since private tenants, many of whom are members of vulnerable households, are badly treated. 3.9% of households in the private rental sector live in over-crowded accommodation – a slightly higher proportion than those in RSLs (3.8%) and 3% of private tenants (compared to 5% of social housing tenants) are unemployed. Nearly a third of households in the private rental sector have no one working in the household.[32] But this is a sector that receives nothing comparable to the financial support, or regulation which the tenants of social housing enjoy. So the reality is that two tenants, in

---

[29] There are some minor schemes worth mentioning. Flats above shops now receive a 100% capital allowance and landlords who rent out rooms in their own homes receive an annual tax allowance of £4250 of gross income.
[30] This means that private landlords have to pay tax on their rental income at a higher rate than other businesses are charged for revenues they raise (subject to corporation tax rates).
[31] Wilcox op. cit. Table 69. p. 162.
[32] Office of the Deputy Prime Minister (2002b). *Housing Statistics Summary: Survey of English Housing Provisional Results: 2001-02.*

otherwise comparable personal and financial circumstances, will have access to properties of very different standards, at very different rents and with very different levels of security, simply because one is in social housing and the other is in the private rental sector. One will (usually) have the right to buy their property at a substantial discount, the other will have no such right. It is also unfair that private landlords – the vast majority of whom are providing a valuable, indeed essential, service – are treated far more punitively by the tax system than are home-owners.

This distortion is inefficient since it eliminates the possibility of any genuine competition between the different forms of tenure. The distorted treatment of tenure types means that if one has sufficient funds to afford to do so then home-ownership will almost always be the most favourable option. For those on low incomes, becoming a tenant of the council or a housing association will usually be the preferred option – offering rent levels, security of tenure and the best possibility of buying one's own home. The private rental sector will therefore inevitably be a 'residual' sector – in the main only attractive in the short-term or for those who are moving frequently.

The generous subsidies and regulated rents available in the social housing sector generate excessive demand for this type of accommodation. But with the supply of social housing heavily limited due to its public expense, it must therefore be rationed through the use of waiting lists, stringent means tests and assessments of 'need'. This ensures that access to social housing (and council housing in particular) is heavily stigmatised and that it is a tenure polarised by the (enforced) dominance of low income households.[33] For this reason it has become strongly associated with unemployment, social disorder and deprivation. At the same time, because gaining access to social housing is so difficult, once a household has attained it there is very little reason for them to move if they can avoid doing so. This has knock-on effects for the mobility of households in social housing, including, for instance, their willingness to move areas to find work. It also has an effect on their willingness to improve their status or raise their household income which may trigger a re-assessment by their landlord. With many social housing tenants effectively 'willingly captive' by their status, the incentives

---

[33] Kemeny, J. (1995). *From Public Housing to the Social Market*, p. 17.

of managers and owners of social housing to maintain standards and treat their tenants fairly and appropriately are insufficient.

Meanwhile, because the private rental sector is penalised relative to both home-ownership and social housing, demand is artificially low. Together with its status as a residual sector, this means that many tenants at the lower end of the sector are effectively captive, since they would exit to either home-ownership or social housing if they could afford to do so. This captive status allows private landlords in some cases to exploit their tenants, and in other cases merely to provide a poor standard of accommodation at relatively great expense, often paid for through housing benefit.

Wasting Public Money

One of the most important reasons for considering substantial reform to the current structure of housing provision is that there are good reasons to think that public money is being wasted. That is, there are attractive alternative financing models which could achieve the same (or similar) social outcomes but at a substantially lower cost.

In order to see this, it is worth dwelling on how the pattern of subsidies has developed over time. A rough summary of the history of public subsidy in housing would be as follows.[34] Prior to substantial state involvement in housing, most people rented housing from private market providers. However, at some point it emerged that the market price for rental housing was such that a significant number of low-income households could not afford a decent standard of accommodation.[35] The solution the government chose to pursue was two-fold: to provide its own substantially subsidised rental accommodation (council housing), and to impose rent controls on private providers. The initial effects of these interventions were to generate tremendous demand among low income households for council housing and to drive out of the market a substantial number of private landlords who

---

[34] For a useful overview of the history of housing policy since the war see Timmins, N. (2001). *The Five Giants: A Biography of the Welfare State.*

[35] The causes of this were partly general and economic and partly to do with the higher standards and regulations that were imposed on new building in response to perceived public health problems with slum areas.

could either not compete with the rents offered by the council, or could not make a profit on the controlled rents they were able to charge their tenants.

Thus the market for private renting was gradually decimated and a huge demand for council housing was spawned. However, predictably, the government's ability and willingness to house everyone who wanted a council home was limited. So, over time, waiting lists grew and the standard of new accommodation was reduced in order to increase numbers. Gradually, the government came to realise that it could not cope with the demand for rental accommodation and so would have to start to remove some of the restrictions from the private market (the inspiration for the 1957 Rent Act, the first attempt to deregulate private rents). One of the consequences of this deregulation was that many low-income households who could not get access to council housing (for whatever reason) turned to private rental providers. Now, these private landlords knew that many of these tenants had nowhere to go (they could not afford their own home and they clearly couldn't get a council home), so some of the unscrupulous landlords took advantage of their situation to charge rather a lot for poor or even terrible conditions (the emergence of Rachmanism).[36]

Another problem emerged: that many of the people could not afford the rents being charged in the private sector. So the government had to intervene to help these tenants by providing them with an income subsidy (rent rebates). The tenants were relieved now to be able to afford their rent, and the private landlords were happy since they knew that the state would meet (virtually) whatever rent they decided to charge.

What has happened, in effect, is that the state's emergence as a mass landlord, coupled with the imposition of rent controls effectively destroyed any proper market in modest rental accommodation. By providing substantially subsidised rents, the state generated a demand for rental accommodation which it could never meet. So there would always be households who would be unable to access council housing. And as public finances deteriorated, and the political appetite for financing council housing decline, this class of people has grown substantially. Thus, those landlords operating outside the state-run system would often be in a

---

[36] In many ways the situation is analogous to the emergence of black markets in goods, existing alongside the state run and price-controlled provision in the former Soviet Russia.

position to exploit their tenants and drive up prices because the state had effectively destroyed the discipline that a competitive market provides.

In terms of public finances this situation is extremely expensive because the state is effectively footing the bill not only for the substantial rental subsidies within council (now social) housing, but is also having to pay more than necessary for the income subsidies necessary to support tenants in social housing and the private market. We can get some sense of how badly we spend public money on housing by comparing how much we spend with what we get relative to other countries. We spend around 3.3% of GDP on housing, compared with 1.8% in France, 1.4% in Germany, and 0.98% in Spain. The only country which spends more is Sweden (4.1%). And, as I pointed out above, this high level of public expenditure has not generated a healthy expansion and renewal of the housing stock. Rather, much of it has been wasted in the process of destroying the market in rental accommodation and then having to subsidise the incomes of those forced back into the market with the retraction of the state as a major landlord.

I would suggest that instead of pursuing this strategy a superior alternative would have been as follows. Low- income households should have received a (cash) income subsidy, set at the level necessary to meet a modest market rent. The recipients of these subsidies would still have an incentive to economise on their housing choices and the providers would face the disciplines present in a competitive market to keep rents at a reasonable level. Over time, as general affluence rose, supply expanded and technological innovations produced cost-reductions, the need for income subsidies, and therefore the public cost, would have declined. Instead, because of the disastrous way we have chosen to support low-income households, the result has been that our expenditure on housing (including expenditure on social housing and housing benefit), rather than falling, has remained stubbornly high.

Conclusion

The UK housing market is suffering from the side-effects of a century of mass state provision of subsidised rental accommodation. There is little competition between the different types of tenure because they are treated so differently in terms of taxes and subsidies. It is not a level playing field, but rather a playing field which is tilted towards home-ownership at one end, and social housing at the other. Current low levels of house-building and investment are another major factor which contributes to affordability problems. The government is alive to some of these problems. We shall examine some recent policy developments in the next chapter.

Chapter 2

Recent Government Policy: Home-Ownership Where Possible, Social Housing Where Necessary

In the last chapter I argued that the main problems in the provision of housing concern, on the one hand, building levels and the responsiveness of supply, and on the other hand, the distorted relationship between the main types of tenure. But what has the government been doing about these problems? Do recent policy developments hold out the prospect of improvement or are they likely to make matters worse?

The government's policy innovations can be summarised under four main headings: the planning system and building levels, home-ownership, private renting and social housing.

The Planning System and Building Levels

In terms of the planning system and new building, two recent developments are particularly relevant: *The Planning and Compulsory Purchase Bill*, and *The Sustainable Communities Plan*[37].

The Planning and Compulsory Purchase Bill, currently going through Parliament, emerged from the 2001 Planning Green Paper: *Planning: Delivering a Fundamental Change.* Unfortunately, following critical interventions by the Select Committee on Transport and a range of criticisms from interest groups[38], many important proposals from the original paper have been either watered-down or dropped altogether. However, some significant proposals remain. From the perspective of housing supply the most important changes concern alterations to the hierarchy of planning.

---

[37] Office of the Deputy Prime Minister (2003). *Sustainable Communities: Building for the Future.*
[38] See Barclay, C. (2002). *Research Paper 02/81: The Planning and Compulsory Purchase Bill* for some details.

22

Under the current system the government issues Regional Planning Guidance after consultation with the relevant regional assembly and the public. At the moment these assemblies are simply the planning conferences, with a majority of members from the local authority and the rest from a variety of different public and private organisations. Should regions opt for their own regional assembly (under separate government legislation) then the elected assembly will assume the planning role. Beneath the regional level is the Country Structure Plan (prepared by the county council), and below that is the Local Development Plan (LDP), which contains detailed specification of the intended use of land.

Under the new system Regional Planning Guidance has been replaced with a Regional Spatial Strategy (RSS), and country structure plans have been abolished. The RSS is to be monitored and implemented by the Regional Planning Body (RPB) – the regional assembly, in consultation with the relevant local authorities. The Secretary of State will remain in complete control of the RSS. The idea is to ensure that central government can impose specific requirements on the regions, e.g. in the form of requirements for new building – a matter that has often been a source of disagreement in the past.

LDPs have been replaced with Local Development Schemes (LDSs). In the original Green Paper it was proposed that Local Development Plans be replaced by a Local Development Framework that would be 'criteria-based' rather than 'area-based'. The idea behind this is that it would make the formation of the plan quicker. However, this proposal has been dropped so that the differences between the LDS and the LDP are now very hard to make out. The most significant change is therefore the abolition of county structure plans.

That this is likely to lead to a dramatic change in the efficiency or speed of the planning system seems doubtful. There will now be a significant gap between the RSS and the LDS – making the process of translating the RSS into an LDS more difficult. And with the LDSs being hard to distinguish from the original LDPs, one could, at best, expect a minor improvement in timeliness and efficiency. At worst the transition to the new system will be a further barrier to timely future planning decisions.

The intended effect of the Bill is 'to speed up the planning system' and, as we have seen, it seems unlikely to achieve that. However, it's not only the speed and efficiency of the planning system that is in question, but also more generally, there are questions about *how* the planning system works and what it is used to achieve. In particular the Bill does nothing to undermine the 'plan-led' nature of the system. That it is 'plan-led' means that proposed developments will continue to be assessed in terms of their consistency or otherwise with the antecedently determined priorities of national, regional and local planning authorities. One of the clear intentions of the Bill is to strengthen the ability of the Secretary of State to ensure that national priorities are implemented properly by local authorities. The question then, is: what are these national priorities and how does the pursuit of them impact on the levels of new building?

This question brings us directly to *The Sustainable Communities Plan* ("*The Plan*") which is the most recent statement of central government policy on housing supply. *The Plan* agrees with the contention that there is severe under-supply of housing at present. It states that current projections of household formation outstrip net formation to the housing stock by some 35,000 a year.[39] One of the stated aims of *The Plan* is to bring about the necessary 'step-change' in supply to remedy this shortfall.

Notably, however, *The Plan* not only has clear views of the amount of supply necessary. It also has a clear and specific idea of where new building should take place and what kind of development it should be. *The Plan* identifies four specific 'growth areas' where new housing should be located: Thames Gateway, Milton Keynes, Ashford, and London-Stansted-Cambridge. This housing must be built at densities of no less than 30 units per hectare and Brownfield sites must be prioritised over Greenfield ones. What's more the government is very specific about what type of housing developments it wants to see. New 'communities' must be 'sustainable' – a vague term which embraces a number of features, including 'strong leadership', 'good quality public services', 'a "sense of place"' and 'good public transport'.[40] It

---

[39] It is important to note that there is ongoing controversy over the government's projections of household growth, with some commentators arguing that they continue to be artificially low. See e.g. Stewart, J. (2002). *Building a Crisis.* for some details
[40] See ODPM (2003) op. cit. p. 5 for a list of the key requirements.

even expresses irritation about the number of 3-4 bedroom houses that are being built in the south-east.[41]

Superficially one might expect that this bodes well for the future of housing supply – a government that has specific concerns about how housing should be built. However, from a historical perspective, there is plenty of reason to question the record of governments in ensuring that the standard and type of building that takes place is of an appropriately high standard. Indeed, the glaring failures of government house-building, from Ronan Point to the soulless council estates of the 1960s, are a testament to the continuing failure of government to deliver high quality and attractive new homes and residential areas. Even today it is clear that the most attractive homes and residential areas are typically the product of the relatively unconstrained efforts of commercial builders, rather than of government-directed development.[42] It is this historical perspective which makes the government's claim to be the guardian of high standards in building and development ring hollow.

But whatever the government's credentials as a guardian of high quality development, in any case, it seems unwilling or unable to commit the necessary funds of government agencies to implement its own ideals. This is reflected in two facts that emerge from *The Plan*. First, that the government has no intention of revitalising local authorities as house-builders. Second, that there will only be limited funds available to deliver the government's vision. The government only pledges some £600 million in seedcorn funding over the next three years to produce the new homes it wants in the growth areas. There will also be £1.5 billion for new affordable housing, provided through the Housing Corporation, increasing by inflation over the next few years.

Clearly, this is not the kind of increase in funding which can be expected to bring about a 'step-change in supply'. And without the direct means for

---

[41] See p. 9: "too many large homes are being built when the demand is mainly for small households".

[42] See Bennett, J. (1978). *A Social History of Housing, 1815-1970*, pp. 238-246. Bennett shows that the competitive conditions during the 1920s were such that private enterprise delivered very high quality homes at affordable prices. The average home then cost just 2.5 times the average salary of the industrial worker. Today, the average home costs around 4 times the average salary (which is considerably higher than the average salary of an industrial worker).

fulfilling its aspirations (i.e. substantial funding and/or direct government provision) it seems inevitable that the government will fall back on the only tool it has for influencing development – the planning system. So we can expect the government to make an aggressive and vigorous use of the planning system in an attempt to enforce these standards of minimum densities, use of Brownfield land, and attributes of 'sustainability' on new private developments. On top of this we have the increasingly extensive reliance of local authorities on the use of planning obligations to increase the provision of 'affordable' (i.e. subsidised) accommodation. It is inevitable, then, that private builders will be subject to more and more extensive constraints and increasingly excessive use of planning obligations. So rather than a 'step-change' or increase in housing supply over the forthcoming years it is more likely that housing supply will remain static or even fall.

However, this is not to say that the construction firms or private developers are likely to suffer greatly from the government's plan-led approach to the provision of housing. Indeed, the substantial constraints on new development generally serve to benefit the big house-builders whose considerable land banks (often ensuring a virtual local monopoly on housing development) ensure that they are in a very strong position to profit from any future developments, regardless of the government's restrictions. Indeed those restrictions generally serve to limit the competition from other, smaller developers. They also enable the builders to keep supply down, ensuring higher prices than would otherwise be possible. The primary losers of the plan-led system are the small players in the construction business and, of course, those on low or modest incomes who do not own their own home.

Overall, the net effects of the Planning Bill are hard to determine at this stage, but it seems doubtful that any significant change to the speed or efficiency of the system will occur. The transition to the new system will in itself be very likely to reduce its speed in the short-term. The gap between the RSSs and the LDSs could easily prove hard to bridge. Most significantly though, there is no fundamental reform of *how* the planning system works - that is, the fundamental policies and guidance of the government which the planning authorities are seeking to implement. This is reflected in the highly prescriptive *Sustainable Communities Plan*. *The Plan*, with its extensive prescriptions but minimal financial commitments, is a recipe for

26

an aggressive and obstructive planning system, thereby serving to keep building levels low.

Home-Ownership

In 2000 the government took the important step of abolishing Mortgage Interest Tax Relief – a benefit that was for a long time seen by the left as a costly subsidy to middle-class home-owners. But this was not the sign of a government committed to substantially eroding the benefits to home-owners. New Labour remains a strong advocate of what it calls 'sustainable home-ownership'[43], meaning home-ownership which is feasible over the long-term. As we will see, the policies have been more problematic than the seemingly unobjectionable epithet 'sustainable' would seem to suggest.

To this end of 'encouraging sustainable home-ownership' the government has outlined a commitment to continue the Right to Buy scheme, although the recent draft *Housing Bill* outlines long-trailed proposals to restrict it in areas where there is a perceived lack of social housing.[44] It has also introduced a number of new schemes to promote home-ownership, most notably the Starter Home Initiative. This scheme, with a budget of £250 million over three years, is devoted to giving £10,000 equity loans to certain 'key workers'[45] in order to help buy their own home. The point of the equity loans is to bring homes which would otherwise be unaffordable for these workers within their reach.

Other subsidised home-ownership schemes include Homebuy (introduced in 1999), Conventional Shared Ownership (CSO), Do-it Yourself Home-ownership (DIYSO) and the Cash Incentive Scheme (CIS) (introduced in 1989). Homebuy is a scheme aimed at encouraging tenants of RSLs to buy their own homes by offering them an equity loan of 25% of the market value of their home, repaid on sale. CSO, a scheme also run by RSLs, allows households to purchase an equity share (typically 25-75% of the value) in

---

[43] Office of the Deputy Prime Minister (2000). *Quality and Choice: A Decent Home for All.*
[44] The Stationery Office (2003b). *Housing Bill – Consultation on draft legislation.* The government is proposing to extend the qualification period from two years to five years and the period after sale during which repayment might be required from three years to five years.
[45] This is the term used to describe certain public sector workers, primarily teachers, police officers and nurses.

an RSL property and pay rent on the remaining share. DIYSO is essentially the same as CSO except that the property may be any property on the market. It is run by a limited number of local authorities. The CIS scheme is a local authority run scheme which offers council tenants a large grant[46] towards the purchase of their own private sector home.

These schemes are an attempt to respond to what is perceived to be the central problem: a shortage of 'affordable' homes to buy. This 'shortage' means that the government is increasingly keen to give any incentive to existing council tenants to encourage them to vacate the property and move into home-ownership. Thus the Right to Buy scheme (and the associated Right to Acquire) and the Cash Incentive Scheme are means of encouraging the better-off social housing tenants to exit their properties and buy their own home. On the other hand, the 'shortage' of social housing has led the government to introduce new government-subsidised schemes to cater for those outside the social housing sector, such as the Starter Home Initiative and the Shared Ownership Schemes. The government's general policy seems to be to erode council housing, and instead to help low or modest income households buy their own home.

These schemes do not, it seems, achieve what they are set out to achieve, since research has shown that considerable numbers of the people helped through the subsidised home-ownership programmes either end up having trouble affording their own mortgage repayments, or even have their new home repossessed. Recent research commissioned by the ODPM reveals that "16-17% of LCHO buyers nationally could not really afford the purchase they were making"[47]. Around one in five of those on the shared ownership or CIS schemes were facing payment difficulties with regard to their mortgage and rates of repossessions for shared-ownership properties were running at nearly four times the national average.[48] The report also found that "30% of shared owners are in some sort of arrears with rent or service charges"[49] and from the available data the authors suggest that a significant number of shared ownership resales resulted in the owners "moving directly

---

[46] Up to 80% of the Right to Buy grant in the south-east or £10,000 elsewhere.
[47] Office of the Deputy Prime Minister (2002a). *Evaluation of the Low Cost Home Ownership Programme.*
NB: LCHO is a generic term for all existing government-subsidised home-ownership schemes.
[48] National rate in 2000/01 was 0.21%. Rate for shared ownership schemes was 0.77%.
[49] Ibid.

or indirectly into social renting". The picture that emerges is of a number of households being encouraged to buy their own home, with the commitment later proving burdensome or unaffordable. Those that can't keep up with repayments faced repossession and/or the prospect of returning to social housing.

It's important to remember that these results are the outcome in a relatively benign macroeconomic environment with low unemployment and falling interest rates. The consequences in the event of a period of recession or rising interest rates could be very severe. Many of these households are clearly not well suited to the particular risks and responsibilities associated with home-ownership, and the government is ill-advised using public money to encourage them to make financial commitments they cannot meet. Contrary to its espoused intention, the government is effectively subsidising 'unsustainable home-ownership'. Potentially this is a mis-selling scandal of catastrophic proportions.

The more serious objection to these schemes is that they will do nothing whatsoever to tackle the underlying problems. Any subsidy to would-be home-owners will increase demand for home-ownership and, without any corresponding expansion in supply[50], simply boost prices further, and worsen affordability problems more generally. Without any measures to increase the levels of new building subsidies merely push prices higher. So the public money will only benefit the direct recipients while worsening affordability problems for other people.

The only substantial policy change that the government has implemented which might be conceived as a move in the direction of remedying the bias in favour of home-ownership has been to increase stamp duty[51]. However, stamp duty hits home-owners and private landlords equally, so it does nothing to rebalance that relationship. In addition, it has been convincingly argued that increases in stamp duty of that kind tend to exacerbate, rather than alleviate house price volatility.[52] Increasing stamp duty is also likely to have a detrimental impact on labour mobility since it means that

---

[50] And, *pace* the first section, such expansion is very unlikely.
[51] Since 1997 the rate for properties from £250K-£500K has been raised from 1.5% to 3%, and the top rate from 2% to 4%.
[52] See e.g Andersen, A., Robertson, D and Scott A. (2000). *Property Securitisation in the UK.*

transaction costs are higher, so people are less willing to move from their properties, and 'trade-up'. Overall, stamp duty is a tax which exacerbates rather than remedies the main problems associated with the housing market.

In summary, the government has done nothing substantial to challenge the privileged position of home-ownership in the housing market. Indeed its considerable range of subsidised home-ownership schemes are arguably an effort to make home-ownership even more attractive relative to other tenures than it already is. The increases in stamp duty will merely serve to worsen volatility and labour immobility and will do nothing to reduce the underlying forces driving demand. The likely effect is therefore that the problems of mass home-ownership - macroeconomic instability, labour immobility and the financial risk to low income households - will worsen rather than improve as a result of the government's policy.

Private Renting

The 2000 Green Paper seemed to hold out the prospect that the government would end the historic maltreatment of the private rental sector at the hands of successive post-war governments. There, the objective was described as "to secure a larger, better-quality, better-managed private rental sector"[53]. Concrete reforms that have emerged seem generally devoted to improving standards, but little has been done that is likely to expand the supply of privately rented accommodation.

The government has recently outlined proposals for licensing of the sector in its draft *Housing Bill*. These include the compulsory licensing of Houses of Multiple Occupation (HMOs) and selective licensing of landlords in areas of low-demand where there appears to be exploitation of tenants. The Department for Work and Pensions have also been piloting a new housing benefit system aimed at reducing fraud and giving greater incentives for tenants in the private rental sector to 'shop around'. Indications from the 2003 Budget seem to be that these pilots will, in time, be extended nationally and into the social housing sector.

---

[53] Office of the Deputy Prime Minister (2000). *Quality and Choice: A Decent Home for All.*, ch. 5

In the Green Paper the government claimed to be 'considering' other measures which might help to stimulate the supply of private rental accommodation, including perhaps a tax free investment vehicle. Some reforms to VAT have been made, for instance giving exemptions for the renovation of flats above shops and stamp duty exemptions in deprived areas. However, renovation remains subject to VAT, unlike new build. In addition, as mentioned above, the government has increased general levels of stamp duty on property transactions substantially.

Overall, the government has not substantially reduced the tax burden on private landlords nor made it easier or more attractive for institutional investors to expand their investment in the sector. As mentioned above, raising stamp duty is likely to make housing transactions more volatile and to deter investment in the sector. The minor reforms to VAT, while a step in the right direction, are unlikely to make a significant difference to the overall attractiveness of becoming a private landlord.

In terms of licensing, while it is right that the government takes action to prevent the illegal or anti-social behaviour of landlords and their tenants, it is not clear that licensing of the type proposed is the appropriate means for regulating the sector, or ensuring that standards are maintained. Crucially, licensing *per se* will be very unlikely to expand the number of good quality private landlords and, given the complexity and costly nature of licensing, it seems likely to deter rather than to encourage the responsible landlords that currently exist within the sector.

So if supply does not expand - it is in fact likely to fall given the government's policy changes - and with little reason to think demand will change substantially, we can expect that rent levels within the private rental sector (particularly within the market for HMOs) will increase. This will exacerbate affordability problems, putting further pressure on housing benefit, and the demand for government subsidised accommodation - either to rent or to buy.

In general little has been done to improve the status of private renting in the UK housing market. At the bottom end it will remain the option of last resort for vulnerable or low income families, and affordability for those households is likely to get worse.

Social Housing

Since 1997 the Labour government has continued and encouraged the transfer of council housing to RSLs. It has set a target of transferring 200,000 homes each year. However, it has also made clear that it wants to raise standards within social housing. The government set itself a target of bringing all social housing up to a 'decent standard' by 2010 and £2.8 billion has been set aside for the next three years to help achieve this.[54]

Overall the government has increased investment in social housing through the Housing Corporation's Approved Development Plan and local authority grants. Gross social housing investment rose from just over £4 billion in 1997/8 to £4.8 billion in 2001/2.[55] There are further planned increases to around £6.5 billion by 2003/04[56]. But increasingly, the government has made clear that money available for social housing has been made conditional on housing being transferred to an RSL or to an Arms Length Management Organisation (ALMO).

The government is pursuing the restructuring of rents in the social housing sector over a ten year period. The aim of the restructuring is to harmonise the rents charged in comparable council properties and properties in RSLs and also to ensure that rents paid reflect the size, attractiveness and local earnings in the area. It is also experimenting with choice-based lettings procedures aimed at increasing the influence social housing tenants have over their accommodation.

Many of the reforms are steps in the right direction. The role of councils as landlords is gradually being eroded through the transfer process and the Right to Buy. Increasingly, as rent-restructuring begins to bite, transfers to RSLs can be expected to accelerate.

However, there remain significant concerns about the government's overall strategy for social housing. First, where transfers do take place the council's local monopoly on social housing is effectively replaced with the RSL's local monopoly. This is unlikely to generate necessary incentives for RSLs to raise

---

[54] ODPM (2003) op. cit. , p. 15.
[55] Wilcox op cit, p. 145.
[56] ODPM (2003) op. cit., p. 66.

standards and drive up efficiency. Social tenants should have the power to exit to another provider of social housing and government subsidy should follow the tenant, not the provider.

Second, little has been done to improve the mobility of tenants in social housing. The structure of social housing continues to foster labour market inflexibility by making transfers difficult and failing to enable current or would-be employees to move nearer to their employer. In 1998 Hughes and McCormick found that, even controlling for other factors such as age and socio-economic group, tenants in local authorities were extremely immobile - some 50 times less likely to migrate than private tenants. [57]

Finally, the net impact of the government's strategy to maintain social housing rents 'well-below' market rents has not been evaluated seriously. As discussed in the last chapter, this strategy generates excessive demand for social housing and drives out of the private providers of rental accommodation. Together with the unavoidable rationing of social housing, the result is huge waiting lists and a residual fall-back by many vulnerable households on an expensive and insecure private rental sector, or the financial risk of home-ownership. A reappraisal of the purpose of social housing and its relationship to the other tenures is necessary.

Summary

The government is continuing the process of removing local authorities as large-scale house-builders or landlords, encouraging those who can afford to buy their own home to do so, and maintaining an independent social housing sector for those who cannot afford to buy. The private rental sector is still seen as a transitional sector, not one which could offer a satisfactory long-term alternative to households. House-building will not be carried out by local authorities nor substantially by housing associations, but will be mainly the task of private builders, under direction from central government. However only small amounts of government subsidy will be

---

[57] Department of the Environment Transport and the Regions (2000). Housing Research Summary Number 136: Housing Policy and Labour Market Performance.

available for the new building and there are few signs that the planning system will become speedier or more amenable to private development.

The government's ideology can be summarised as "Home-ownership where possible, social housing where necessary". It has continued the historic bias in favour of these two tenures and has shown no interest in fundamental reform of the relationship between the three main tenures. The likelihood, then, is that the problems outlined in the previous chapter will worsen rather than improve as government policy is implemented. New housing supply will remain unresponsive and at inadequately low levels. The result will be continuing medium and long-term house price inflation, with worsening macroeconomic instability, widespread affordability problems and financial risk to low income households. These trends, in turn, will fuel demands for further and further subsidies to home-owners and social housing tenants, at the expense of the private rental sector. It's time to consider a different way of doing things.

Chapter 3

A Different Model: A Social Market in Housing

In the previous chapter I hope to have explained some of the problems with the housing market as it operates in the UK, and the principal causes of those problems. I also argued that the direction of government reform is unlikely to improve things substantially and may make matters worse.

I argued in Chapters 1 and 2 that the persistent problems facing the housing system in the UK stem from the following main facts:

- The failure to maintain a reasonable level of new build over the past 20 years.
- The distorted treatment of the three main types of tenure, which artificially encourages people to opt for either home-ownership or social housing, and has tended to eliminate healthy competition from the private rental sector.

I also argued that recent government policy reforms are unlikely to have any substantial impact on these problems and may even make matters worse. This analysis suggests that solving these persistent problems involves some radical changes to forces influencing the supply of housing and the relationship between the tenures.

A. The Planning System and Building Levels

As we saw in Chapter 1, there is persuasive evidence that a good deal of the house price inflation in the past twenty years or so has been caused by woefully low levels of new building and investment – levels which seem to be evidence of a clear failure of the market to expand to meet supply.

In the housing market, it is therefore particularly important that a steady stream of new building is maintained, in order to prevent excessive inflation of prices over the medium and long term, which will lead to serious affordability problems in time. How can this be ensured?

The discussion of the problem in Chapters 1 and 2 argued that current low levels of building are primarily due to:

- The sluggish and burdensome planning system
- The inability of housing associations to gain access to land
- Government restrictions on private developers
- The incentives for land owners to drip-feed, or withhold land
- The volatility of the market.

In terms of the planning system it is clear that the current system is not working, and very doubtful if the proposed changes will substantially improve matters. In particular, the most obvious problem is that the system remains 'plan-led'. That is, unlike other domains of government regulation, government sees its role not as merely providing the overall framework within which free development can take place. But rather, it appears that the government sees the proper role of the planning system as being to actively shape and direct development according to government priorities. And this is where things become difficult. For those government priorities, embodied in the planning system, can then often become an obstacle to the goals which ordinary developers want to achieve. There is therefore a real question to be asked: given that the economy is no longer 'planned' in any significant sense, and that the vast majority of developments in housing are to be provided by private developers, does planning for housing really makes much sense? A plan-led system simply doesn't fit with private development.[58]

Thus, in the medium to long term the objective should be to effect a shift, as far as possible, from the role of the planning system as specifying what land *can* be used for to what, in broad terms, it cannot be used for. The role of the planning authorities should be to specify in generic terms what would not be a permitted development and then, beyond this, to allow the market to provide the answer as to what *should* be built. And, of course, it is essential that specifying what's not permitted does not become overly stringent (cf. the Green Belts).

---

[58] It is as if the government was to attempt to 'plan' how many banks there should be in any given area, zoning some areas as 'in need of a bank' and others as 'bank-full', and trying to use these specifications to influence the location of new banks.

In the short-term a reasonable alteration would be for the government simply to stop planning for housing supply. That is, it should stop trying to estimate the amount of housing that is 'needed' and then to attempt to use the planning system to ensure that it is built in the amounts and types desired. Not only are there good reasons to think that the government isn't good at determining these types of questions,[59] it is even clearer that it has no hope of delivering the objectives without the re-emergence of substantial public funding for new build – a prospect that has probably never been less likely.

Provided that there is not severe harm to the environment or a detrimental impact on the locality, private developers should, in the main, be allowed to provide the amount, type and size of houses they wish to build. Developers should be allowed to meet the actual demand for housing, rather than the government's view of what provision should be. So any targets or quotas for affordable housing should be abandoned, and section 106 agreements should not be used for that purpose. During the inter-war years (when planning was almost non-existent) private developers achieved tremendous output, without sacrificing standards, and housing was much more affordable as a result. In that situation the affordability of housing was a result of strenuous competition between construction companies, high levels of building, and decreasing costs. It was not the artificially state-subsidised version of 'affordability' which the government seems currently keen to pursue.

But to remove the artificial constraints on developments is not the only change necessary to boost supply. It is also necessary to tackle the incentives of private developers to hold land, or 'drip-feed' it to the market. As discussed in earlier chapters, the current system is failing to deliver the appropriate level of new build partly because the volatility of the market serves as a deterrent to expanding output.

One policy suggestion to tackle this problem would be to impose a tax on land values, on all unused or unproductive land. It could be applied to all unused land which either had existing planning permission for new build, or

---

[59] I am thinking here both of the poor record of 'predict and provide' as a strategy in the post-war era and also of the commonly noted tendency of governments in recent times to provide very inaccurate forecasts of household growth.

was not already zoned for some other purpose. This would be an effective means for increasing the supply of land during times of booming prices, since the owner would face an escalating tax bill. Correspondingly, in times of slump, owners of land would not be penalised since they would see their tax burden fall. The tax could be refundable should the land be used to develop housing. Such a tax would tend to reduce the extreme volatility of land prices, and increase the supply of land for housing.

More generally, though, it is the volatility of the housing market which really needs to be tackled if supply is to be improved. Only when house price inflation is less erratic and more predictable over the medium to long term will house-builders expand supply.

The government, in particular the Treasury, is alive to the problem of housing market volatility, reporting both that "housing market imbalances are a potential break on economic development"[60] and that "reducing volatility in the housing market will...promote macroeconomic stability".[61] These are major concerns for the government in relation to the convergence criteria for monetary union. However, the government's main efforts in this area have been confined to raising the levels of stamp duty, and recently, to discuss the possibility of expanding the market in long-term fixed rate mortgages.[62] However, raising stamp duty will probably worsen volatility rather than improve it and there is no obvious market failure in the provision of long-term fixed rate mortgages.

Part of the solution to the problem of volatility lies in removing some of the artificial incentives that exist to become a home-owner, in particular in the promotion of a healthier and more attractive rental market (of which more below). This would provide a valuable buffer to the housing market and be likely to reduce the amount of debt tied up in housing. But, a full solution almost certainly lies in setting a property tax on home-owners which is proportional to the (imputed) rental income of the property. Such a property tax would have the same effect on the housing market as a land value tax would have on the land market. As house prices rose, home-owners would have a greater incentive to sell, rather than hold on to their

---

[60] HM Treasury (2003). *The Budget 2003*, p. 71.
[61] Ibid, p. 42.
[62] Ibid, p. 43.

property, but when values fell, so too would the tax-burden and therefore the incentive to sell. In both cases, the effect would be to stabilise fluctuations in prices. This tax is used in a range of other European countries, including France, the Netherlands, Sweden, Belgium and Spain.

B. Tenure Neutrality

A steady supply of new building is one important precondition of a healthy market in housing, but it is not the only one. Another condition is to ensure a relationship between the three main tenures which will have the effect of maximising fairness and efficiency.

I argued in Chapter 1 that a persistent theme of government policy has been to privilege both home-ownership and social housing over private renting. The result has been that there has been excessive demand for home-ownership and social housing has been insulated from competition with other providers. At the same time many low-income households have been forced into the private rental sector due to the necessary rationing of social housing. This system is inefficient, since competition between the tenures has been minimal. It is also unfair since government subsidy has tended to follow the *type of tenure* of housing, rather than the *consumer or recipient*.

What is needed, therefore, is to start to remedy this bias in favour of home-ownership and social housing, replacing it instead with a more neutral framework within which all providers of housing must compete with each other on a broadly level playing field. This is a framework which many have called 'tenure neutrality'.

Such a framework is attractive on the grounds of efficiency, since if it is neutral between providers, all providers will have an incentive to raise standards in order to gain a competitive advantage. It is therefore the best means for generating an overall increase in standards, to ensure that failing providers go out of business and that good providers can expand.

Such neutrality is attractive on grounds of equity too. A liberal state should not aim to impose the preferences of one class of individuals on all members of that society.[63] If one's preferences are unreasonably penalised by state activity, that is unfair. In housing this means, for instance, that even if most people prefer home-ownership to renting, that is not sufficient reason to use the apparatus of the state to artificially advantage the former over the latter. It also means that those who rent privately might reasonably resent the position of (otherwise comparable) tenants in council housing who often enjoy a standard of accommodation, security and rent which is unavailable to those in the private rental sector.

Unfortunately, tenure neutrality has been very far from being a guiding principle of housing policy in the UK. The promotion of subsidised council housing and home-ownership over private renting has been a persistent theme of the last 60 years in housing policy. This has led to a situation in which people are artificially forced to choose between either social housing or home-ownership, when, for a large class of people, private renting would be the favoured option if it was a better developed market, and treated as well as the other two tenures. That renting is not inherently less attractive than home-ownership is illustrated by the large and flourishing rental sectors that exist in other European countries. Nearly 70% of people in Switzerland choose to rent privately, and the rate is 36% in Germany, and 21% in France, compared to just 10% in the UK.

So What Does Tenure Neutrality Mean in Practice?

The principle of tenure neutrality applies to both the ownership and the provision of housing. All *owners* of housing, whether they be home-owners, private landlords, or not-for-profit landlords, ought to be subject to roughly the same regulatory and fiscal regime unless there is a good reason to treat them differently.

At the moment houses owned by private landlords are treated as a form of investment under the tax system, but houses owned by home-owners are treated as ordinary consumption goods. This is unfair because home-owners are profiting from their investment just as much as private landlords. The only difference is that private landlords are renting to whoever will pay the

---

[63] This idea is extensively discussed in Rawls, J. (1999). *A Theory of Justice* and Rawls J. (1993). *Political Liberalism.*

rent, whereas home-owners are only 'renting' to themselves or their family! What this means is that individuals are given an artificial incentive to live in, rather than rent out, the kinds of properties they can afford to buy. The consequence is therefore that people who can afford to rent a property, would almost certainly be better off buying it, making renting inherently inferior to home-ownership.

Tenure bias in terms of taxes and subsidies is particularly harmful between home-owners and private landlords because of the phenomenon of tax breaks being capitalised into house prices. Economists often argue that because the supply of housing is relatively fixed in the short-term tax breaks will tend to be capitalised into house prices, that is, merely raise house prices by the (discounted) net present value of the tax break. In other words, the tax break merely results in higher prices (benefiting existing owners), but does not alter the affordability of housing for would-be buyers. And because private landlords must also compete in the same property market, such tax breaks also have the effect of raising prices for them, which causes higher rents for private tenants. Any tax break for home-owners will inevitably, if indirectly, penalise private landlords and their tenants.

So if we were to institute tenure neutrality between private landlords and home-owners both would be subject to capital gains tax, and home-owners would also be subject to a tax on their imputed rental income (as private landlords are taxed on their actual rental income). However, both would also be eligible for interest relief and an allowance for maintenance expenses.

C. Responsible Renting and the Role of Not-for-Profits

Nonetheless there remain good reasons to think that neither home-ownership nor private renting will be the optimal form of housing provision for everyone. One of the main reasons for this concerns the nature of housing as an essential good which people place great value upon and which is often difficult and costly to exit (sell or move out).

When one lives in a house for any length of time it often becomes something more than a house – rather it is a home - something we are emotionally attached to, that we would not wish to give up, perhaps the only home our children have ever known[64]. This means that as we live somewhere for a period of time, we typically become less willing to move. This is also because there are usually substantial costs to moving. This is typically not so for our consumption of other goods and services.

If we are renting the property, this raises the problem of potential exploitation by the landlord. Although most landlords are primarily concerned with maintaining their rental income, and also lose when there is a change of tenancy, it is undeniably a temptation for any landlord to, say, raise the rent of a household who is becoming attached to their home and unwilling to leave. A profit-maximising landlord may well have an incentive to raise the rents of households whom he perceives are reluctant to leave their home. But, and this is strongly intuitive, many of us would see this as exploitative or unfair in some respect, particularly if the household concerned has a low income, or is vulnerable in some other way. Sentiments like this are one major reason for believing some form of social housing or home-ownership to be inherently superior to private renting.

This is where not-for-profit organisations, mutuals and cooperative providers of housing can play a valuable role in bringing a range of non-commercial instincts to the provision of housing. A not-for-profit organisation (such as a housing association) can allow a more flexible approach to the treatment of its tenants, permitting non-commercial elements to influence their thinking, in a way that a private, profit-making company may find difficult to countenance. A not-for-profit organisation can, for example, use as a unique selling point that it offers particularly long leases to families, or that, after a probationary period, households are guaranteed tenancy for 5 or more years. It can also afford to be less ruthless about short-term downturns in profitability, and give a higher regard to 'human capital'.

The key idea here is not that not-for-profit organisations of a variety of kinds are likely to be the only responsible and attractive providers of rental accommodation. Rather, it is that the presence of such organisations in a competitive market, offering their services to a wide variety of households,

---

[64] Of course one may get sick of living there too, but the phenomenon of a house becoming a home is widespread and important.

could act as an important disciplining force on all providers, whether for-profit or not-for-profit. Not-for-profit organisations could act as *market leaders* in rental accommodation – determining the standards and costs which other providers must follow.

Private, shareholder-based providers may be better at raising private capital, being innovative and driving down costs. On the other hand they are less likely to be consistent and responsible providers when financial circumstances become difficult. Not-for-profit organisations are likely to be less able to raise capital, will be less commercially orientated and expansionary. But they are more likely to maintain standards when the going gets tough. The ideal – the social market – lies in trying to ensure that both types of providers can co-exist in a dynamic and creative tension.

This tension, and the competition that results, ideally leads to for-profit rental providers being leaders in terms of the *quality* of accommodation, and not-for-profit providers being leaders in the provision of *inexpensive* accommodation. Each sector can benefit from the competitive pressure of the other.

A number of changes would be necessary in order to bring about this competitive market between for-profit rental providers and not-for-profit rental providers. First, it is necessary to ensure that existing council properties are transferred to RSLs as quickly as it is feasible to do so. To this end, the government should set a deadline for all outstanding council stock to be transferred to RSLs – say 18-24 months from now. The government should also insist on a policy of no new council house tenancies. As tenancies expire, instead of new tenancies being awarded, councils should sell the property to a local RSL. If necessary, the government could consider providing an incentive for tenants to opt for an early transfer e.g. offering a sum of up to 1% of the market value of the property for those tenants which opt for an early transfer.

Second, the government should cease providing capital subsidies to RSLs. The vast majority of the stock is now such that rents can be charged at a modest level, without the need for capital subsidies, because levels of debt are not prohibitively expensive. The solidity (the ratio of free equity to market value) of the sector as a whole appears to be well above the level necessary for it to effectively compete with the for-profit rental sector. The asset value of the RSL housing stock stands at £54.6 billion compared to net debt of only £18.7 billion[65], giving the sector a solidity of 66%.[66] This compares with a probable optimum solidity of 30%. So the lesson is straightforward. Even if the sector as a whole continues to substantially increase the levels of debt, the financial position is such that they could easily compete with for-profit rental providers. Indeed their position is such that RSLs could keep rents at modest levels (below the levels offered in the private rental sector) without the need for either government subsidy or statutory restrictions on rent increases. As RSLs assume more debt, they can use their ability to cross-subsidise to keep rents down on newly acquired properties.

Third, RSLs should be freed up from extensive control by the Housing Corporation and local authorities. Many of these controls are, wrongly, put in place to ensure not that RSLs must compete with private landlords, but rather to ensure that they don't have to, since in many ways they are continuing to perform the role that council housing once played. That is, many RSLS are to a large extent being used by government agencies as simply a form of off-balance-sheet council housing. This is, of course, particularly true of RSLs which have absorbed transferred council stock. In exchange, they are insulated from the competitive pressures involved in the rest of housing market.

Instead, RSLs should be permitted, indeed encouraged, to expand their provision into new areas. Rather than being confined to the role of providing 'housing for the poor', they should aim (and be permitted) to provide modest rental accommodation for anyone who wants it. The proper relationship between RSLs and private landlords should therefore be akin to the relationship between building societies and banks. That is, their different status as institutions is acknowledged in the fiscal and regulatory structure, but not in a way that undermines the ability of the two types of institutions to compete. Instead in many ways, the two types of institutions should compete for the same market (or markets which overlap), but do so, in ways which appeal to different types of people.

---

[65] Source: Housing Corporation and National Housing Federation (2003). *Global Accounts of Housing Associations Part A.*

[66] Solidity = Free Equity / Asset Value = (£54.6-£18.7) / £54.6 = 66%.

In order to bring this about, it is important that the government does not artificially disadvantage private landlords over RSLs or vice versa. What this means is that over time, the aim should be that they become subject to broadly the same fiscal and regulatory structure. At the moment private landlords pay capital gains tax, tax on their rental income and stamp duty. RSLs pay none of these taxes and indeed receive capital grants and loans from the government.

D. Housing for Those on Low Incomes

In the UK historically it has been thought that council (now social) housing would be the primary answer to the problem of how those on low incomes can be ensured access to a satisfactory standard of housing. For those on the left, it has traditionally been thought that since those on low incomes are often unable to exercise market choices, or pay market rents, they would only be able to enjoy a decent standard of accommodation if it was provided, at substantially subsidised rents, by government agencies. Private renting was thought to be unsuitable since it was deemed inherently expensive, insecure and exploitative. Those on the right tended to agree with this analysis and to accept the need for council housing, but also saw the state as having an important role in helping those on low incomes to become home-owners.

Council housing has since lost favour across the political spectrum, with all major parties agreeing to continue the transfer of council homes to housing associations, believing that the latter are more responsible and effective landlords, while also being able to generate private capital off the public sector balance sheet. Councils tended to be very variable in quality as landlords, enjoying a local monopoly in the provision of subsidised housing, which made it difficult for tenants to exit should they be unhappy with the service they were receiving. Plausibly it could be argued that the monopolistic position of councils in the provision of housing actually allowed them to be irresponsible and, to some extent, exploitative, landlords.

So how do we ensure that all families have access to a decent standard of accommodation in a social market? According to principles of the social market, providers of housing will be most likely to maintain standards if consumers have the option of exit – can freely move to other accommodation if they are dissatisfied. Crucially, this applies not only to the wealthy, but also to those households with modest or low incomes. Providers of social housing will also be more likely to provide good value accommodation if they must compete against each other for tenants. They will be even more likely to innovate and drive down costs if they must also compete with profit-making landlords and home-ownership as tenures. This is another reason for supporting the principle of tenure neutrality – it is an important safeguard for households with low incomes. Fair competition drives prices down and standards up, benefiting low-income households as much, if not more than, the better off.

If tenure neutrality is established and all providers of housing are competing on a level playing field, the value of available housing will be maximised. However, it remains very plausible that even in such ideal conditions some households will lack sufficient funds to afford a reasonable standard of accommodation. What to do?

The most obvious answer is that the government should redistribute income to those households in order to bring their incomes up to the appropriate level. Here, tenure neutrality requires that we assess the level of housing allowance to which households are entitled not by the type of housing in which they live, but by other features of the household, principally according to the size of the household, its level of income, and the market price of accommodation in an area. The household could then decide whether to use the allowance to subsidise a mortgage, or a private rent, or a cost rent.[67]

There would nonetheless be many reasons to think that a disproportionate number of low-income households would favour renting from a not-for-profit organisation such as a housing association. This is because such households are typically also lacking in the necessary assets (e.g. a deposit) to gain access to home-ownership. They are also more likely to place a

---

[67] Special considerations, nonetheless, will apply to the case of low income home-owners. A low income home-owner is in a fundamentally different situation to a low income household in rental accommodation, and different considerations apply, for instance, the ability of the household to release equity through sale, or re-mortgage. However, the levels of assets of low income households in rental accommodation may also be an important determinant of the level of housing allowance available.

higher value on security of tenure over flexibility, than those on higher incomes, generally making a not-for-profit provider the most-attractive option.

However, there are good reasons for preventing not-for-profit renting from becoming exclusively the domain of low-income households. When this happens the sector becomes stigmatised, and rightly or wrongly, associated with a range of ills including unemployment, social disorder and crime. It thereby becomes unattractive to tenants from a range of income groups. This is when not-for-profit renting becomes 'ghettoised'. This, arguably, is what has happened in the UK.

The main reasons for this happening are the restrictions on the subsidies going to councils and housing associations and the 'needs-based' assessments for access to social housing. While council housing has traditionally been nominally available to anyone, the existence of substantial waiting lists ensure that local authorities, and derivatively most housing associations, have had to introduce their own allocation criteria to determine the priority of different households. Typically different households are given a certain number of 'points' based on an assessment of their 'need', with those with the greatest need going to the front of the queue. This, in conjunction with substantial restrictions on the ability of local authorities or housing associations to expand their capacity, means that, by and large, only households with very low incomes, or in severe deprivation can get access to social housing. This ensures that the sector is increasingly ghettoised. Households more likely to be in work, or with higher incomes are thus increasingly excluded from social housing, and given the unattractiveness of private renting, tend to see home-ownership as the only attractive option in the long-term.

A radical solution to this problem would simply be to jettison the system of waiting lists and allocation based on 'need', entirely. Arguably it is the very cause of ghettoisation and stigmatisation – in short a contributor to 'social exclusion'. If all providers of not-for-profit housing were statutorily obliged to take all tenants regardless of 'need', based simply on 'ability to pay the rent' and 'suitability for tenancy',[68] the result would be to open the tenure up to all types of households, not just the most deprived.

But would the result be that the households genuinely in need of housing would be deprived of it, while middle-income or well-off households benefited from the lower rents? This is only likely to be the result if the amount of social housing is artificially limited. Otherwise, provided that the housing allowance paid by the state to low income families is at a sufficiently high level, providers of social housing (or indeed, private rental providers) will expand in order meet the demand.

If there is a fear that housing providers will try to 'cherry-pick' middle-income households rather than take perhaps higher risk lower income families, then one intervention the state could consider would be to offer all providers of rental accommodation a special premium for housing recipients of housing allowances. This would tend to even-up any tendency of landlords to favour better-off low-risk households over low-income high-risk households.

Another important question is: Should RSLs be permitted or required to charge below-market rents? The problem with very heavily subsidised rents being offered in the domain of social housing, and not others is that it is anti-competitive – a form of 'dumping' which drives out other providers of rental accommodation. And because such housing is always limited in quantity, rationing is necessary, with the attendant problems of arbitrariness associated with this. This means that those who can afford to wait will eventually get it, but others may be forced to resort to private renting, or taking the risk of home-ownership. This allows providers of accommodation outside the social rented sector to exploit their tenants whose option to exit is limited. On the other hand, if providers of social housing can't charge below-market rents, what is the point in their existing?

The sensible answer is to ensure that providers of social housing are statutorily obliged not to distributes profits, and have a commitment to expanding the availability of good value rental accommodation (as they do

---

[68] Allowing landlords to refuse tenancy to say, a family, they had reason to believe would be violent, unruly or disruptive.

already), but nonetheless allow them to set their rents freely, within these constraints.

Not-for-profit providers would *naturally* see their role as involving using cost-savings and revenue surpluses to help them reduce rents (whereas profit providers might use revenue surpluses to distribute to shareholders or pay off debts). If there is reason to think that they are not pursuing their 'mission' then their favourable tax status can be withdrawn. But a statutory blanket restriction on rents in the social housing sector will harm competition from the private rental sector and to some extent constitute an unreasonable restriction on the ability of the sector to ration demand fairly.

The experience of rent controls in the UK has been that they generally have the effect of driving landlords out of the market, reducing supply and generating new problems of access for those on low incomes. In addition, rent controls, once instituted, almost invariably become difficult or impossible to remove because of the political cost of doing so. A preferable model is not to use rent controls, but to rely on the appropriate incentives being put in place for both landlords and tenants to keep costs down, and drive standards up. If the right market structure is in place, and income subsidies to low income households are in place, rent controls will be unnecessary. What's more, the expectation ought to be that, over time, the cost of income subsidies will drop as the real cost of housing falls with efficiency gains and economies of scale and as average earnings rise.

A Summary of the Main Elements of a Social Market in Housing

So these are the main elements of a social market in housing:

- No direct state provision
- A liberalised planning system which allows private developers to decide how much and what type of accommodation to build.
- A fiscal and regulatory system which is broadly neutral between all providers of housing, home-owners, profit renting and not-for-profit renting
- No statutory rent controls.
- An important, market-leading role for RSLs.
- Generous income subsidies for low-income households.

The aim of the social market framework is to provide an environment in which there is maximum competition between different providers, allowing all consumers to exit to another provider should they become unhappy with the standard of their accommodation. The market would be likely to include home-ownership, private renting and RSLs, with low-income households afforded generous housing allowances which would enable them to purchase a decent standard of accommodation. RSLs would be the natural, although not exclusive, domain of low-income households.

It is worth at this point reiterating the advantages of this social market approach over the current housing market in the UK. A liberalised planning system, coupled with some system of land value taxation would bring about a substantial increase in levels of new building and investment. Increases in the taxation of home-owners would help to reduce house price volatility, and greater certainty about future prices would encourage private developers to increase output. In the medium to long term, affordability and housing standards would improve.

A more tenure neutral tax system would tend to lead to a bigger and more attractive rental sector and smaller but more sustainable levels of home-ownership. As a result the macroeconomic problems associated with very high levels of debt-financed home-ownership would be alleviated. Also, with a bigger and healthier rental sector it is highly likely that labour market mobility would be enhanced, with a corresponding knock-on effect on unemployment and productivity. Over time, fewer households with low and/or uncertain incomes would opt for the risk of home-ownership but would instead be able to find attractive and affordable accommodation in the rental sector. The financial risk to such households would thereby be substantially reduced.

Overall efficiency in the housing sector is likely to be much better under the social market system. Competition will be enhanced by a more neutral fiscal and regulatory regime. Inefficiencies in the provision of housing will be minimised both through greater competition, and through income rather than rent subsidies. Under the new housing benefit system, households will be able to afford a decent home, while retaining reasonable incentives for them to shop around for the best value accommodation.

The elimination of rent controls and transfer of properties to RSLs will also help to foster competition, and encourage new entrants into the market. With the elimination of rent controls and harmonisation in the treatment of not for profit rental providers and private rental providers, the cost of accommodation to the tenant will be directly related to the standard and attractiveness of the property, eliminating the unfair distinctions between council tenants, housing association tenants and tenants in private rental accommodation. Not for profit renting will no longer be the exclusive domain of low income or deprived households, and stigmatisation and ghettoisation of the sector will be reduced. RSLs will be able to set rents in order to ration demand fairly, while keeping them at affordable levels.

Lastly, but crucially, cost in terms of public expenditure should be reduced over time. Government subsidies will follow households in need rather than institutions or providers. The liberalised planning system will ensure that supply expands and good quality housing becomes more (rather than less) affordable over time. The neutral market framework will ensure that competition between providers is fierce and efficiency is correspondingly high. With expectations of rising levels of prosperity and falling or static real house prices, the burden on the public purse should fall over time.

With the social market system described, in the last chapter, I'll outline an agenda for reform, shifting the UK towards a social market in housing.

Chapter 4

From Here to There

In the last chapter I argued for a different model for housing provision in the UK, based on the idea of promoting greater tenure neutrality between the main types of housing providers. In this chapter I will outline the main policy changes that would be necessary in order to help effect the shift to a social market in housing.

Unfortunately it has not been possible to calculate the fiscal impact of the proposed changes. However, one important point must be noted. The point of the proposed taxes is not to increase the tax burden generally. They are justified simply for the reasons given in this paper, namely in the interest of promoting a fair and efficient market in housing. Where the proposed changes would raise substantial funds or increase net tax revenues an important priority would be to decrease other direct taxes on individuals and households, e.g. income tax and national insurance contributions. I have indicated two taxes – council tax and stamp duty – which, because of their deleterious effects (respectively of being seriously regressive and of exacerbating price volatility) would be a strong priority for abolition.

Another important point to note is that these reforms are generally to be taken as a package, not simply to be taken in isolation without understanding how each fits into the overall plan of generating a social market.

Priority 1: Promoting an Expansion of New Building

There is little hope of a healthy and dynamic market in housing unless the supply problem is first addressed. To this end it is proposed to:

- Introduce land value taxation on unused / unproductive land held by developers.

- Abolish the 'plan-led' system of managing housing supply in favour of using the planning system to specify (only) which areas cannot be used for housing, with the implication that all other areas can be used for housing.

- Abolish requirements for minimum densities, proportions of affordable housing and attributes of 'sustainability'. Only use 106 agreements to provide for necessary local infrastructure.

Priority 2: Improving Provision for Low Income Households

Council housing, and the restrictions placed on RSLs continue to provide an obstacle to the creation of a fair and efficient market in modest rental accommodation. To remedy this and to improve the provision for low-income households it is proposed to:

- Set a deadline for the transfer of council housing to RSLs (18-24 months). No new tenancies should be awarded. As homes become vacant they should be sold on to an RSL.

- Ensure that no RSL has an unreasonable local monopoly on cost renting by requiring transfers to occur to more than one RSL.

- Phase-out all capital subsidies to RSLs and councils.

- Gradual deregulation of RSLs but allow tax exemption for charitable status.

- Housing Benefit Reform: a generous income subsidy, related to household size and local costs, but not actual housing costs. Could eventually be assimilated into general income support.

- Consider setting a housing benefit premium payable to providers of housing for those households in receipt of HB.

Priority 3: Reducing Tenure Bias

Many of the serious problems in the housing market stem from the distorted and unfair relative treatment of home-ownership, private renting and social housing. To remedy this distortion, it is proposed to:

- Introduce (phase-in) 40% Capital Gains Tax on home-owners.

- Introduce an annual property tax on home-owners (based on a proportion of the imputed rental income or market value of the property) - say 1.5% of the market value of the property - with deductions permitted for maintenance costs and interest on debt.

- Abolish council tax.

- Abolish stamp duty on all housing transactions.

- Abolish government-subsidised home-ownership schemes, such as The Starter Home Initiative.

- Over time, seek to harmonise the treatment of private landlords and RSLs making them both subject to roughly the same fiscal and regulatory system.

Bibliography / References

Andersen, A., Robertson, D and Scott A. (2000). *Property Securitisation in the UK.*

Balchin, P. (1996). *Housing Policy in Europe.* Routledge.

Barclay, C. (2002). *Research Paper 02/81: The Planning and Compulsory Purchase Bill.* House of Commons Library.

Burnett, J. (1978). *A Social History of Housing, 1815-1970.* Routledge.

Burrows, R. (2003). *Homeownership and Poverty in Britain.* Joseph Rowntree Foundation.

Department of the Environment Transport and the Regions (2000). *Housing Research Summary Number 136: Housing Policy and Labour Market Performance.*

Department of the Environment Transport and the Regions (2001). *Planning: Delivering a Fundamental Change.*

Department for Work and Pensions, (2002a). *Households Below Average Income 2000/1.*

Department for Work and Pensions (2002b, November). *Income Support Quarterly Statistical Enquiry.*

Department for Work and Pensions (2003). *Family Resources Survey 2000-01.*

The Economist (2002, November 16th). House Prices: British Exceptionalism.

European Union (2001). *Housing Statistics in the European Union 2001.*

FPD Savills (2003, March). *UK Land & Development Research Bulletin.*

HM Treasury (2003). *The Budget 2003.*

Housing Corporation and National Housing Federation (2003). *Global Accounts of Housing Associations Part A.*

Kemeny, J. (1995). *From Public Housing to the Social Market.* Routledge.

Office of the Deputy Prime Minister (2000). *Quality and Choice: A Decent Home for All.*

Office of the Deputy Prime Minister (2002a). *Evaluation of the Low Cost Home Ownership Programme.*

Office of the Deputy Prime Minister (2002b). *Housing Statistics Summary: Survey of English Housing Provisional Results: 2001-02.*

Office of the Deputy Prime Minister (2003). *Sustainable Communities: Building for the Future.*

Oswald, A. (1999). "The Housing Market and Europe's Unemployment: A Non-Technical Paper", available at: http://www2.warwick.ac.uk/fac/soc/economics/staff/faculty/oswald/homesnt.pdf

Rawls, J. (1999). *A Theory of Justice.* Oxford University Press.

Rawls J. (1993). *Political Liberalism (The John Dewey Essays in Philosophy).* Columbia University Press.

The Stationery Office (2003a). *The Planning and Compulsory Purchase Bill.*

The Stationery Office (2003b). *Housing Bill – Consultation on draft legislation.*

Stewart, J. (2002). *Building a Crisis.* House Builders Federation.

Timmins, N. (2001). *The Five Giants: A Biography of the Welfare State.* Harper Collins.

Walker, D. (2002, March 6). Home Truths. *The Guardian.*

Wilcox, S. (2003). *UK Housing Review 2002/2003.* Joseph Rowntree Foundation.

Appendix

Social Markets in Practice

Introduction

Critics of the idea of a social market will inevitably accuse the model of being impractical or politically impossible. The point of this appendix is partly to assuage those fears by providing an overview of some variants on the social market model practised in two European countries, namely Switzerland and Sweden. While neither of these countries exhibits the precise model advocated here, they do possess certain important features which the present UK model lacks.

First, tenure neutrality plays a much more important role in the two systems than it does in the UK. In the case of Sweden, tenure neutrality has been an explicit policy aim for some time, albeit one which has been under attack in recent years. In the case of Switzerland, Professor Philippe Thalmann describes how tenure neutrality, while not an explicit policy aim, has been an important principle underlying tax equity and the allocation of subsidy.

Second, partly as a result of tenure neutrality, renting has been an attractive option for a range of households, and not only for the short term or for those who are unable to afford to buy. Indeed, in the case of Switzerland, private renting can genuinely be said to be the norm. This has been the consequence of a more tenure neutral system, and relatively light rent controls (in the case of Switzerland) and a large not-for profit sector (in the case of Sweden). Neither country has exhibited the positive ideology of home-ownership that has been a persistent feature of recent government policy in the UK.

But both countries exhibit certain problems characteristic of advanced housing markets. In both cases the problems concern levels of new supply which have tended to decline as a result of a heavy and burdensome planning system, declining bricks and mortar subsidies and rent regulation. Increasingly this is having a knock-on effect on levels of affordability and overcrowding, as suppliers become less and less willing to enter the market. An increasingly urgent policy problem these countries face will be how to balance the need to preserve the interests of current home-owners and tenants with those of future generations. A similar problem faces policy-makers in the UK, if in a different context.

In the first section Professor Philippe Thalmann provides a valuable overview of the provision of housing in Switzerland. In the second section Professor Jim Kemeny describes the history and development of the social market in Sweden. Both contributions shed light on how social markets work in practise and of their important merits.

Switzerland

Professor Philippe Thalmann, Swiss Federal Institute of Technology, Lausanne, May 2003

The main tenures in Switzerland

The Swiss housing market may be a variant on the social market model that Tom Startup calls for. Historically the Swiss government neither adopted a *laissez-faire* approach to the provision of housing, nor did it ever become a major landlord.

One striking feature of the Swiss housing market is the very low proportion of households that own their home. This proportion is the lowest in the OECD, at 31.3% in 1990. That compares to owner-occupation rates of twice that size in many other OECD countries. There is, however, wide variation within Switzerland. The owner-occupation rates in primarily urban cantons such as Geneva (13.8%), Basle-City (11.0%), and Zurich (20.9%) are much lower, while rural cantons have rates over 50%. The owner-occupied sector has always been a relatively small part of the housing market.

60

Table 1 Tenure statuses for dwellings of principal residence, Switzerland 1970-90

	1970	1980	1990
Full ownership	25.5	24.2	24.0
Shared ownership	2.4	3.5	2.9
Condominium ownership	0.6	2.4	4.4
Total ownership	28.5	30.1	31.3
Co-operatives	3.9	3.9	3.7
Ordinary rental	63.7	63.0	62.8
Farming lease	0.8	0.5	0.3
Service or free dwelling	3.1	2.5	1.9
Total rental	71.5	69.9	68.7

Source: Aebersold (1994, p. 11)

The earliest data on the share of home-ownership are from a partial census in 1950: 37%. That figure is higher than the rate in the UK, the Netherlands or France at the same time and not much lower than in other European countries. However, all those countries saw their rates grow following the last war while the Swiss rate first declined to 28.5% in 1970 under the influence of strong immigration, then rose very slowly to possibly some 35% in 2000 (data to be published shortly). One important early factor was the legal impossibility, from 1912 until 1965, to buy an apartment in a multi-family unit and, since then, the hurdles placed in the way of the conversion of rental to owner-occupied apartments. Further reasons are detailed in below.

However, the low proportion of home-owners does not mean that few people own real estate. It is quite common for tenants to own a secondary residence or even rental housing. In 1990, 68.8% of all housing units belonged to individuals[69] or 51.5% of all rental dwellings of main residence. However, much of that property is concentrated in the hands of few, with just 9% of Swiss households owning rental dwellings (Gerheuser, 2001, based on a survey in 1998).

As indicated, about one half of the Swiss rental market belongs to individuals. The remainder belongs to property companies, pension funds, insurance companies, co-operatives and foundations. There is no statistical category which clearly identifies not-for-profit landlords, but the following categories of housing providers could be counted as mainly not-for-profit: co-operatives (7.5% of the rental stock in 1990), public sector (3.7%) and foundations and associations (2.5%). The total share of not-for-profit housing is thus 13.7%. Moderate rent regulation protects the other 86.3% of tenants from the odd greedy landlord.

About 10% of the housing stock is built with some form of public aid. However aid is not reserved for needy households or not-for-profit landlords. It is therefore very difficult to clearly identify and quantify social housing in Switzerland. But it would probably not amount to more than 3-4% of the housing stock.

Housing policy

The relatively small size of the owner-occupied housing stock is not at all a sign of poor housing conditions. Its complement is a private rental sector that provides comfortable housing to most households and adequate opportunities to private investors. In comparison to other countries, regulatory interference (e.g. rent control) is moderate and housing policy is fair towards rental housing. The provision of rental housing relies heavily on private initiative. At the same time little is done to promote home-ownership, although the issue is often on political agendas.

In spite of that generally favourable assessment, housing policy is in the process of fundamental revision. Indeed, there are reasons for everyone to be dissatisfied. The Right bemoans the low share of home-ownership and

---

[69] That is the sum of 27.8% owner-occupied main residences, 30.4% rental housing and 10.6% secondary residences, vacant homes and others.

excess rent regulation, while the Left complains about near-permanent housing shortage and a ratchet effect that has rents grow with costs but never decline when costs do.

The present situation is shaped by policies which were set up after the first oil-price shock and the ensuing deflation of a huge construction bubble. Earlier experience with rent control and housing aid also shaped that policy. There are essentially four pillars to current housing policy (Cuennet et al., 2002).

Rent regulation

Wartime and post-war rent control was replaced in 1972 by regulation against 'abusive' rents, comparable to the UK's 'fair rents' system. Basically, rents are abusive if they provide landlords 'excessive' returns. Under that theory, a tenant may oppose the rent she pays and force her landlord to open his accounts and prove that he is not overcharging. In order to reduce uncertainty and litigation, the law sets criteria for raising rents every 6 or 12 months based on changes in typical costs (interest rates and inflation). Indeed, tenants typically challenge rent increases (more rarely decreases that are not granted) rather than initial rent levels. Neither rule allows not-for-profit supply to exert any influence on rent setting via rent regulation. There exists however a third rule, which lawmakers introduced in the law at the request of property interests: a rent is not abusive if it is close to those of comparable dwellings in the neighbourhood. That rule is designed to avoid a growing spread between the rents of new and old dwellings. Although landlords frequently referred to that rule, courts have rarely accepted it due to the difficulty of comparing dwellings.

The government is revising rent regulation, due to growing dissatisfaction among both tenants and landlords. The aim is simplification without sacrificing tenant security. The solution found was to limit allowable rent increases to changes in the consumer price index. But this did not solve the problem of initial rent levels (for rents concluded with a new contract) nor of the absolute level of rents. For this reason, policy-makers considered a system based on the rule of comparable rents. A statistical service would define a set of average rents for all types of dwellings. However, tenant organisations found the system insufficiently transparent and landlord organisations opposed the dissemination of market information. No solution is in view today.

Promotion of rental housing

Two fundamental principles drive housing aid: (1) The market is primarily responsible for providing housing, and (2) public subsidy should be marginal (there is an informal ceiling of 10% of new dwellings aided). Only a small proportion of new build is by public authorities, namely some cities. Rather, federal, cantonal and local authorities grant loans and facilitate private credit rather than handing out non-refundable subsidies. There are no general tax rebates for rental housing, but a few cantons use that instrument for non-profit housing for low-income households.

The primary instrument for promoting the construction of rental dwellings is a schedule of loans designed to lower the initial cost of new housing. The annual loans are reduced over time, and then they are reversed, so that the beneficiary pays back the loans with market interest. The schedule is set up for 20-30 years to make rents, which are then completely controlled, grow with the general trend of prices and incomes. Means-tested and non-refundable subsidies may further reduce charges. The builder may also apply for federal credit guarantee separately from the loan and subsidies. It allows him to borrow at a preferred rate with a smaller down payment.

Support is available for the construction, the purchase and the renovation of housing. Any landlord can apply for support, provided he abides by the terms of the contract with the authorities, including full rent control for 20 to 30 years. Nevertheless, not-for-profit societies (co-operatives, foundations)[70] are privileged partners of the housing authorities. Since they generally lack equity, the authorities help them with special loans. Their tax treatment is not particularly generous. They are taxed like regular corporations with few exemptions, such as no stamp duty on the emission of shares. Not-for-profit housing is by no means reserved to those who cannot afford regular market rents.

---

[70] A society obtains that status if its statutes restrict its activities to building and acquiring dwellings of moderate rents or prices, forbid dividends exceeding 6% of social capital, and provide that residual equity after dissolution of the society be affected to similar use.

The deflation of the construction and price bubble in the early 1990s placed many landlords who were beneficiaries of federal aid in a very difficult situation, preventing them from raising rents and repaying the federal loans as scheduled and forcing the government to stand up for its credit guarantees. In the face of the losses and a slackening rental market, the federal authorities decided to scale back their aid massively and to suppress it completely by 2002.

Starting in 2004, federal rental housing aid will be reserved for not-for-profit landlords. Two thirds of the money will be for renovations and only one third for new build. It will take the form of free or cheap loans directly granted by the government for individual dwellings under conditions of occupation. That strange construct is the result of a compromise between those who wanted direct personal assistance to households in need and those who wanted to maintain aid to construction. Still, local authorities are invited to pay direct personal assistance.

Promotion of home-ownership

Until 2001 the explicit instruments of aid to home-ownership were the same as those for rental housing, namely loans and credit guarantees (Thalmann, 1997). Non-refundable subsidies were never paid out. In the process of revising and focusing housing aid, it was nearly decided to drop federal aid to home-ownership, leaving it to the cantons to decide whether they want to promote home-ownership.[71] But the federal government, in response to a campaign from the rural cantons, agreed to offer similar aid for home-ownership as for rental housing in areas without large rental Taxes paid by the landlord and the tenantmarkets.

Tax treatment of the tenures

In money amounts, the principal support for home-ownership is through tax rebates, even though Swiss tax authorities are not very generous to home-owners. The playing field for the tenures is clearly not as tilted towards ownership as in the UK.

---

[71]   Thalmann (1999) provides arguments for decentralisation.

In order to compare the taxation of owner-occupied and rental housing, we must consider similar situations: a household that owns its home and a similar household that owns a dwelling but rents it to another similar household. Their taxes are summarized in the following table.

Comparison of the taxes paid by a pair landlord and renter with the taxes paid by an owner-occupant

Taxes paid by the landlord[1] and the tenant	Taxes paid by the owner-occupant
Income taxes	
Rental income is added to owner's taxable income	An implicit rental income is added to owner's taxable income
Owner may deduct from taxable income his costs: mortgage interest, maintenance and other expenses	Idem
In four cantons, the tenant may deduct rent paid from taxable income[2]	–
Wealth and property taxes	
An estimate of the property's value is added to the owner's taxable wealth	Idem
In about half of the cantons, the owner pays a complementary property tax; in certain cantons, the tax is higher for incorporated owners; the tax base is the gross value of the property, i.e. without deduction of debts	Idem. Only one canton treats differently rental property and owner-occupied property
Transaction taxes	
The owner pays various rights and duties at the purchase or the sale of a dwelling, mainly transfer and recording duties	Idem, except in two cantons which apply a lower rate to the sale of one's principal dwelling under certain conditions
The owner pays a special tax on capital gain in all the cantons but not at the federal level	Idem, except that the owner who sells his dwelling profits from carry forward of tax in almost all the cantons in the event of reinvestment within a limited period

(1) We suppose that the landlord is a private individual and that the building belongs to his private fortune.
(2) This was introduced in the late 1980s with a view to offsetting tax advantages granted to home-owners. It disappeared recently with federal tax harmonisation.

The table shows that the tax treatment of owner-occupied and rental housing is basically equivalent, implying a system that is tenure neutral in this respect. Indeed, the Federal Court has repeatedly ruled that tax equity takes precedence over the promotion of home-ownership. Nevertheless, practical considerations give the cantons some leeway to favour home-owners, which all use to varying degrees. It is particularly difficult to assess implicit rents for owner-occupied dwellings and the cantons tend to underestimate them. The Federal Court accepts under-estimation by no more than 40% and it can safely be assumed that 30% is the standard. On the other hand, two tax factors play against home-ownership: (1) the landlord may be incorporated or even tax exempt (e.g. pension funds), in which case income taxes are less (but note that more than half of the home-owners declare negative net income from their home after deducting expenses); (2) home-owners pay transaction taxes every time they change residence. Our simulations with real tax data show that home-owners benefit from lower housing costs after four to five years of residence (Thalmann and Favarger, 2002).

Obviously, current tax advantages to home-owners are not targeted at encouraging accession (and even less mobility), since they grow with the length of ownership. Imputed rents are estimated less frequently than changes in rental rates on the market. The assessment of apartments for wealth and property taxes is even less frequent and, in most cantons, a rebate is granted which increases with the length of the holding period. Even the capital gains tax is lower for longer holding periods (to prevent speculative trading). Of course, tax advantages granted beyond the year of purchase are also valuable to home-owners and may influence the choice of tenure. However, households which discount the future attach less value to those advantages at the time of deciding to buy than their cost in current public budgets. Furthermore, any under-estimation of economic income and wealth is more profitable to households in high tax brackets. Those households are not the marginal homebuyers.

The tax treatment of owner-occupied housing is also being revised. The most likely outcome will be the removal of the imputed rent together with the deductibility of interest payments. This is seen mainly as a simplification. Open questions concern the deductibility of maintenance and other expenses, with a view to encouraging proper maintenance, as well as some deductibility of interest for new owners over their first years.

Federal organisation and tenure apportionment of housing policy

The central government plays the leading role as regards the promotion of housing construction and renovation and the promotion of home-ownership. That is not true, however, when tax rebates are taken into account since the federal government, the cantons and the municipalities share income taxes roughly in equal proportions and all wealth, property and transaction taxes are cantonal and local. Some cantons augment federal housing aid. The larger municipalities promote housing for low-income households. Some provide housing themselves. The local authorities have always been very important in implementing national policies.

The federal government allocates funds for aid to rental and owner-occupied housing roughly in proportion of those tenures' shares of the market. Thus, housing aid is in effect tenure neutral, although there is no law requiring that. Full assessment would need consideration of tax rebates to home-owners on the one hand and implicit rebates to tenants under rent monitoring on the other hand.

Housing policy for low income households

Rent control helps keep rents low in the face of housing shortage. It is not particularly targeted at low-income households though and may even place them in a very difficult situation when they must change residence. More effective aid is provided in the form of means-tested income assistance, which is basically the sum of an allowance for rent, an allowance for health insurance and an allowance for other expenses. The larger cities build housing directly or through not-for-profit foundations that they try to reserve for lower-income households. There are, however, long waiting lists for those dwellings, in part because tenants whose economic conditions improve are rarely made to move out. So in effect income assistance often picks up the rents for standard market housing.

Eligibility for income assistance and reduced-rent housing is based on self-registration and self-reporting of income and wealth. There exists not special treatment for the unemployed.

Performance of the housing market

Most aggregate indicators of housing market performance are quite satisfactory. Housing expenditure has been growing quite steadily but slowly from about 12% of total consumption at the end of the War to some 16% today. That was accompanied by steady growth in comfort, measured in particular by surface per dwelling and even more in terms of surface per inhabitant. In general the housing stock is in very good shape, with standards for rental dwellings that exceed the standards for condominiums in many European countries. The price of that comfort is high though, with rents far exceeding the levels in neighbouring countries in spite of a long history of low interest rates. Indeed, Switzerland is in first position of all European countries as regards the construction cost of its dwellings. A standard family dwelling costs between 6 and 7 times the median annual income. Even higher income families that buy their dwelling spend 5.5 times their annual income (Thalmann and Favarger, 2002)

There are swings in house prices as in other countries. Between 1970 and 1989/1990, the average price of single-family houses offered in newspapers grew by a factor of 3.5 while the CPI grew by a factor of 2.3. Then house prices declined to 75% in 1998 of their peak value, while the CPI grew by a further 25% (Swiss National Bank data). The swing in rents for dwellings offered on the market was even more pronounced, with a peak in 1992 at 4.5 times the 1970 level, followed by a downswing by a third until 1999 and strong recovery since then. However, that does not concern all dwellings. The rent index for all occupied dwellings has grown more or less regularly to 3.3 times its 1970 level.

The incredible swing in rents for dwellings offered on the market is the result of a supply of new dwellings almost never able to keep up with demand. Since the end of the last war, the proportion of vacant dwellings never exceeded 2% and it exceeded the 1% mark only in two periods: after the first oil-price shock and in the second half of the 1990s. In 1990, just before the index for rents offered on the market peaked, the vacancy rate was only 0.44%. There were virtually no vacant dwellings in the larger cities. Such a situation is recurring these days.

Low vacancy rates are clearly the main problem for most households, particularly of course for those that arrive on the market or must move. Fortunately, it does not express itself in homelessness but rather in long waiting lists and inadequate densities (crowding and under-occupation).

The responsiveness of house-building to demand

That vacancy rates can fall below 1% and stay there for several years is strong evidence that house-building is not very responsive to demand. Just now, Switzerland is traversing a very paradoxical situation with vacancy rates falling from a (small) peak of 1.85% in 1998 below 1% today and new building also falling to historical lows. The 31,000 dwellings built in 2002 are only 0.86% of the stock, a ratio never seen since in fifty years of statistics. The current situation is thus quite similar to that in the UK in that levels of new building are clearly unresponsive to changes in demand.

Private builders carry the main burden of construction in Switzerland and they have cut back their activity. They blame excessive regulation of the market (rents and contracts), which thwarts adequate returns. In fact, regulation is much less strict than in many neighbouring countries and it did not get any stricter recently. But there is clearly increased uncertainty due to the current difficult overhaul of housing policy mentioned earlier. Tenant associations point at investors who go after quick profits on the financial markets; but the recent downturn of those markets did not help construction.

Land is certainly a key factor in explaining construction levels, as in the UK. Switzerland is a small country that tries to protect its landscape through a demanding planning system. In theory, there is sufficient land set aside for housing construction. In practice, builders find it very difficult to locate adequate land, owners willing to sell and local authorities disposed to provide the additional infrastructure and to authorise building. Those hurdles are particularly high for large projects, so that no large housing estate has been built recently which is comparable to those that helped face rapid population growth in the 1950s and 1960s.

The social status of the different tenures

A large survey of Swiss households in 1996 showed that a majority of them dream of home-ownership (Thalmann and Favarger, 2002). In fact, most of them combine an aspiration for home-ownership with a desire for detached housing, which puts that dream even further out of reach. So there is this pull factor for home-ownership. However, other standard pull factors such as the protection against economic instability, access to better neighbourhoods, a higher social status or important tax advantages hardly exist. What are missing most are the push factors. In repeated survey, Swiss tenants have expressed great satisfaction with their housing conditions and even with the rents they pay.

As a result, there is not the same sharp social divide between renters and home-owners as in other countries. Many higher income households are very happy in long-term private rental - a rarity it seems in the UK. One fifth of the tenants report gross yearly income above CHF 120,000 (Gerheuser, 2001), which is about twice median household income. Econometric analysis of our 1996 survey (Thalmann and Favarger, 2002) shows that by far the main determinant of ownership is the desire to own one's home, and that desire is only weakly correlated with income and wealth or other personal characteristics, except children and age (retired persons very rarely dream of home-ownership). Income and wealth are nevertheless direct determinants of home-ownership. In a nutshell, the likelihood of a household to own its home is higher when it strongly desires such ownership, when it is married, when it is wealthy, when it is Swiss and when its head is independent rather than salaried and over 40 years old. The median age of moving into ownership is 35 years, the mean 38. Fifty-eight per cent of all home-owners live in a single-family house as compared to 6% of all renters.

Almost one half of the households surveyed could not pay down the standard 25% deposit out of their own equity. Standard lending conditions provide for slow amortization to about 60% of the property's assessed value. So Swiss owner-occupants are relatively highly indebted, accounting for a ratio of private household mortgages to GDP of about 75%. That is clearly a reflection of the long tradition in economic stability and growing property values. Nevertheless, the surprisingly sharp increase in interest rates in 1989-1990 put many recent home-owners in difficulty, leading to foreclosures, a marked decrease in prices and losses for lending institutions in the billions.

Concluding assessment of the current system

The Swiss housing market has enviable features. Tenants and home-owners express great satisfaction and do not call for fundamental changes. The small proportion of home-ownership need not be a problem and could even be a plus point in the face of business cycles and geographic reshuffling (see the 'Problems of Mass Home-Ownership' in Chapter 1 and Thalmann, 1997). Even the low vacancy rate can be seen as evidence of efficient management of the housing stock.

Nevertheless, housing policy has become an intricate mesh of sometimes contradictory instruments and rules over the last 30 years. Reforming that mesh is proving extremely difficult in the face of many vested interests. Nevertheless, such reform and a clear result are urgent, if only to restore sufficient predictability that will encourage investors to address pent-up housing demand.

Specific categories of households face particular hardship on a tight market. Relief is sought in income support and some public housing provided by local authorities. Federal support allows for better burden sharing. Our analysis of household budgets shows that only some 4% of all renter households face hardship because of adverse housing conditions - they pay excessive rents (Thalmann, 2003). They are the prime candidates for targeted housing aid. The other 17% of all renter households whose income is not sufficient for basic needs after they paid their rent actually need general income support rather than housing aid.

The country must urgently address the difficult choice between expanding the housing stock to meet all desires for more housing surface on the one hand, and protecting the remaining green fields on the other hand. Rent regulation is fine if it stabilizes rents over the business cycle, not if it keeps rents below economic costs over the long run in spite of continued housing shortage. More realistic rents and fewer tax barriers to mobility would allow re-equilibrating the market without a non-sustainable expansion of the housing stock. If the concern is that landlords benefit from excess returns thanks to housing shortage, rent regulation could use the rents charged by not-for-profit providers as a reference.

As a general matter, not-for-profit housing providers could assume a greater leadership role: in catering for low-income and special-needs households, in providing a steady flow of new building, and possibly in setting the reference for rent regulation or providing a market leading role. To that end, public authorities should provide them greater support, mainly in the form of credit and access to land.

References

AEBERSOLD A., *Miete oder Eigentum? Die Oekonomische Entscheidung über Wohnungsbesitz*, Dissertation, University of St. Gallen, 1994.

CUENNET, S., P. FAVARGER AND P. THALMANN, *La Politique du Logement*, Collection Le Savoir Suisse, Presses Polytechniques et Universitaires Romandes, Lausanne, 2002.

GERHEUSER F. W., *Mietbelastungen, erweiterte Eigentümerquote, Wohnverhältnisse und Wohnzufriedenheit*, Bericht z.H. des Bundesamtes für Wohnungswesen, Büro für Politikberatung und Sozialforschung, Brugg, 2001.

THALMANN P., 'Housing policy towards ownership in Switzerland', in : BACCHETTA P., WASSERFALLEN W. (eds), *Economic Policy in Switzerland*, Macmillan, Basingstoke, UK, pp. 214-242, 1997.

THALMANN P., 'Which is the appropriate administrative level to promote home-ownership?', *Swiss Journal of Economics and Statistics*, vol. 135(1), pp. 3-20, 1999.

THALMANN P., 'Measuring housing affordability by having regard to housing and household conditions', *mimeo*, 2003.

THALMANN P., FAVARGER P., *Locataire ou propriétaire ? Enjeux et mythes de l'accession à la propriété en Suisse*, Presses polytechniques et universitaires romandes, Lausanne, 2002.

Sweden

Professor Jim Kemeny, University of Uppsala, Uppsala, Sweden, May 2003

Introduction

Sweden has pursued a model of housing provision similar to that advocated by Tom Startup. Tenure neutrality has been explicit government policy for a long time. The aim has been to allow demand to determine supply and hence the relative size of the tenures. The way this is achieved is complex but, in essence, all loans, for whatever purpose (home-ownership, not-for-profit renting or for-profit renting), are tax-deductible, while all capital gains realised through sales are taxable. The result has been that while home-ownership constitutes a significant proportion of the housing stock (approx. 45%), there is a flourishing and attractive rental market for those who want it (accounting for around 40% of the housing stock).

The rental market is unitary[72], meaning that not-for-profit and for-profit rental providers compete on roughly equal terms, the result being that neither sector is merely the preserve of the poor and that not-for profit rental providers exert significant pressure on the rents and standards of accomodation in the profit-rental sector. How this has been done is discussed in detail below. Not-for profit rental providers account for slightly more than half of the rental market, with the remainder owned by private for-profit rental companies and private individuals. Most of the latter own at least one apartment block. There is also a modest tenant-ownership stock of apartments - some 16 percent of the total stock.

Partly as a result of tenure neutrality, the housing stock is highly stratified by tenure and dwelling type. There are almost no houses - whether terraced, semi-detached or detached - that are available to rent, nor are there any owner-occupied apartments. One consequence of this is that owner occupation is dominated by households with children and there is much more movement from owner occupation back into both renting and

---

[72] Here I refer to the distinction between 'unitary' and 'dualist' markets, which I introduced in my *From Public Housing to the Social Market* (1995).

tenant-ownership, especially after children leave home, than is the case in English-speaking countries. This is primarily a move from suburban owner occupation to inner city apartment living.

The Swedish housing market enjoys some enviable features over the typical housing markets in English speaking countries, and in particular in the UK. With a system approximating tenure neutrality and an attractive rental sector, individuals are not artificially forced to opt for either home-ownership or social housing (not-for-profit renting). Sweden does not have the sort of macroeconomic instability that has plagued the UK because fewer people own heavily-mortgaged homes so fewer people are directly affected by changes in interest rates. Housing markets are somewhat less catastrophic, with individuals able to find relatively attractive rental homes where they need to settle.

Low income households are well catered for by a large not-for-profit rental sector which offers decent permanent rental homes at very high housing standards and at affordable rents. The need for income subsidies is much less than in the UK and other English-speaking countries. Importantly, not-for-profit providers are not confined to a role as 'providers for the poor', but in fact cater for a wide range of household types. So although there are clear social differences between areas, the sector as a whole does not suffer from the kind of extreme stigmatisation and ghettoisation which has been a feature of the model pursued in the UK.

The Swedish model, however, has not been an unqualified history of success. In particular, it has faced difficulties in achieving progress towards a fully integrated, free, social rental market, in which not-for-profit rental providers can exert effective market control over profit-providers without the need for regulation. I provide a historical overview of some of these problems below.

Background

Before the Second World War, Sweden's rental market was a traditional unregulated profit-driven market dominated by private landlords. Gunnar Myrdal, then Minister of Housing, was a key player in opening the market to competition from not-for-profit housing organisations following a major commission of enquiry into housing. The decisive factor behind this was the inability of the profit rental sector to provide sufficient cheap housing for ordinary people, and the need for alternative providers. The immediate trigger was the flight of capital from housing to the munitions industries that took place with the outbreak of war. But the malaise was, as in most societies, chronic.

The path chosen by most English-speaking countries - that of creating a publicly-owned "poor-housing" sector, thereby keeping the rental market as a sheltered reserve for profit-seeking landlords - was eschewed in favour of nurturing not-for-profit providers to eventually be in a position to compete in the open rental market on equal terms with profit-providers. The hope was that shortfalls in housing construction on the part of profit-providers would be made up by not-for-profit providers. In turn, not-for-profit providers would be able to expand their market-share until they could comprise an effective competitor to profit-renting, providing not-for-profit housing for a wide range of households.

Rent regulation and interest subsidies, 1942-1967

To achieve the aim of producing a not-for-profit rental sector which could become an effective player in the market it was necessary to provide government support for not-for-profit providers, while minimising discrimination against for-profit landlords. This was done by making available housing loans at subsidised rates of interest to both for-profit and not-for-profit providers. But while those to for-profit providers only covered 70 percent of construction costs those of not-for-profit providers were for 100 percent. The thinking here was that the established for-profit landlords would normally have capital reserves to draw on or potentially mortgageable property to raise loans with. By contrast, the new not-for-profit providers did not have either the capital reserves or the loan potential. In addition, rent regulation was designed in such a way as to ensure that costs were covered as well as allowing a margin for profit. As each annual cohort of newbuild aged, its rents were raised to cost-covering levels plus a margin for profit. This meant that the rents of for-profit and not-for-profit housing were kept in line with each other. However, as construction prices rose and as the housing stock grew, a rent gap emerged between old and new buildings.

Historical cost rent regulation (called in Sweden "rent-splitting") was introduced in 1942. As the years passed the rent gap between old and new properties grew. As it grew, demand became increasingly skewed towards older and lower-rent properties. It is well known that old properties are not intrinsically less attractive than new ones - quite the opposite in many cases. They are usually more centrally located and are often thought of as having "charm" (*the bijou factor*) - constructed in old styles, with high or sloping ceilings, tiled stoves, *etc.* Therefore, a black market quickly emerged in which tenants paid key-money to gain access to centrally-located charming old rental property with low rents.

De-regulation: (1) from rent-splitting to negotiated rent-setting: after 1967

The move towards the social market was accellerated when, in 1967, rent-splitting was replaced with a new system of negotiated rents based on the principle of use-values. Each year rent levels are negotiated between the tenants union and SABO, the not-for-profit national umbrella organisation. Once these are determined, for-profit providers then have to set comparable rents, thereby giving not-for-profit a "market-leading" role. Comparison is, of course, made with similar not-for-profit housing, which presupposes a good representation of not-for-profit rental housing in all segments of the market. It should be noted, however, that "market-leading" in this context is achieved through the system of indirect regulation (negotiated rent-setting) not through the exercise of market strength. This system therefore fell short of a free social rental market.

The idea of having the tenants union negotiate rents with the not-for-profit companies was to provide a check against unreasonable rent increases. The tenants union was to act as a sort of watchdog to ensure that in the absence of the profit motive to drive them, the not-for-profit housing companies remained cost-conscious. Perhaps uniquely, in the Swedish case, the tenants union was therefore given a key corporatist role in rent-setting. However, one of the problems with such a negotiated rent-setting system is that the tenants union are not only concerned to keep rents low. They argue that their existing members should not have to cross-subsidise newbuild for future tenants, but rather that newbuild should be subsidised by society as a whole.

77

While research findings do indeed show that the demand gap between older attractive apartments and newer less attractive apartments did decrease, negotiated rents did not significantly reduce the distorting effects of rent-splitting. Older properties continued to have lower rents than newbuild, despite being generally more attractive. Since 1967 there has been further market-based reform of this system to give greater consideration to locational factors (which the tenants union have been resisting). But the system still favours the tenants of old properties and the black market in the rental contracts for older properties remains.

De-regulation: (2) the maturation of the social rental market since 1967

Progress towards an integrated social rental market has been painfully slow but nevertheless discernable. Much of the tardiness has reflected the enormous expansion in housing demand that took place in Sweden in the early decades of the postwar period - Sweden's era of urbanisation. Not-for-profit housing organisations provided the great bulk of this output. This in turn kept their front-end loading very high throughout the 1940s and 1950s, culminating in the "million programme" from 1965-1974 when one million new units were constructed. By the late 1970s, the ratio of outstanding debt to market value was still not much less than 1:1.

By the end of the million programme not-for-profit rental housing had reached numerical parity with for-profit renting. However, due to the sustained heroic levels of newbuild, its ability to cross-pool rents remained significantly below that of the for-profit sector. It is only the decline of overall levels of newbuild sustained over the last quarter of a century that has enabled the outstanding debt-to-market value ratio of the not-for-profit stock to gradually fall to significantly below 1:1.

In Sweden this ratio is an important measure of competitive efficiency and is usually termed *solidity*. A solidity of 30 percent indicates a debt burden amounting to 70 percent of the market valuation of the housing stock. This is commonly taken as an optimum level of solidity and one that is often found in the older and more slowly-expanding for-profit rental sector. Once the not-for-profit rental sector reaches these levels of solidity it will reach parity with the for-profit rental sector in terms of its financial competitiveness.

An analysis of the solidity of the not-for-profit housing organisations carried out by SABO in the early 1990s indicated that in the major urban local authorities solidity had risen to around 15 percent. In the twenty years since then, low rates of newbuild in combination with rapidly rising property prices have undoubtedly increased their solidity even further.

Increasing solidity has been reflected in further de-regulation. Since the early 1990s, not-for-profit has been exposed to the same taxation and subsidy regime as for-profit rental providers. Even more important, all interest subsidies were phased out and by the turn of the century net housing support was more than outweighed by net housing taxation. Not-for-profit providers are now to all intents and purposes treated no differently from for-profit providers.

There are some exceptions, the most important being that - in constrast to for-profit providers - not-for-profit providers are still expected to meet the housing needs of the disadvantaged. However, as mentioned above, they are not confined to a role as 'providers for the poor'. In addition they are still essentially local operators; that is, owned by the local authorities and their market activities are restricted to within the boundaries of one local authority, while for-profit operators may operate wherever they like.

Recent retrograde developments

Recent events have undone some of the progress made in the previous half-century. The first is that a bourgeois coalition local government (Stockholm City) implemented a sort of right-to-buy in the period between coming to office in 1998 and losing it in 2002. The attractive inner-city not-for-profit rental stock disappeared as large-scale conversions of not-for-profit to co-operative tenant-ownership were made. As a result of this, the not-for-profit share fell between the two local elections from around 20 percent to 5 percent. The Stockholm government also transferred - some 4 billion kronor of housing assets - from the not-for-profit housing company, *Stockholmshem*, to the local government holding company. Effectively this was an example of large-scale asset-stripping.

The new social democratic Stockholm City government has stopped the sales but much damage has already been done. There have also been other sell-offs. In one (Greater Stockholm local government), where a bourgeois government took control, the entire not-for-profit stock was sold to a for-profit landlord. In Malmö the not-for-profit company lost its not-for-profit status when the local government took out too high profits. As a result of all this and similar cases elsewhere, not-for-profit rents - as the basis to compare to for-profit rents - are getting hard to find in some areas.

These, of course, are local changes that are usually associated with the election of a bourgeois local government. As such, the effect remains patchy and varied. Cities like Gävle and Uppsala have not had a change of government and so have not experienced this sort of asset-stripping. Stockholm is, of course, a major market and, moreover, one that is attracting in-migration from rural northern areas. Yet, as the Stockholm experience testifies, it only takes the election of a local government that is hostile to not-for-profit renting for much damage to be done to the move towards an integrated rental market in just one mandate period.

Central Government attempts to prevent asset-stripping

The social democratic central government is trying to protect the not-for-profit companies from this sort of erosion but its not clear if they will succeed. For example, they want the locally-owned not-for-profit rental companies to be made into housing associations with protected status instead of as at present being companies under each local government holding company (koncernföretag). This would prevent one-off elected local governments from assest-stripping them either by selling them or exposing them to political decisions like right-to-buy. Another damage limitation measure is to require that all proposed sell-offs of not-for-profit stocks be subjected to review by the county in which the housing stocks are located. Those sell-offs would then only be approved if they do not so decimate the not-for-profit stock as to seriously compromise the ability to set profit rents by reference to local not-for-profit alternatives.

The other change has been that because negotiated rents continue to skew demand towards older properties, there is now little new-build investment. This has become an increasingly acute problem, and should probably have been dealt with earlier by further relaxing of rent-setting procedures.

Sweden is thus facing a similar low levels of new build and investment to the UK, albeit for somewhat different reasons.

But rent-setting procedures have not been relaxed. Instead, the Tenants Union, SABO and the Private Landlords Association have recently come to their own agreement that newbuild should have free rent-setting, and the government has agreed (a particularly clear case of housing policy corporatism). The trouble with this change is it is going to have a rent-splitting effect – a return to the 1942-67 model, though in a new variant. What is needed is market-sensitive rent-pooling so the cost profile of the not-for-profit stock imitates the market while remaining within cost-covering limits.

One problem here is that the tenants union always looks to its members' interests first, which means protecting existing tenants at the expense of future tenants. So it has been fighting a rearguard action against market-simulating the not-for-profit rent structure, and trying to maintain as much historic cost rents as possible. They argue that existing tenants should not have to subsidise newbuild through rent-pooling (rent-averaging) – this should be the government's rsponsibility in subsidies paid for by everyone. The latest "iron triangle" agreement is in line with that aspiration.

Concluding Remarks

The Swedish experience is that progress towards a fully functioning and free social rental market has been at best crab-like (or perhaps more like two steps forward one step back). One solution would be to phase out negotiated rent-setting in selected local markets where there are strong and well-established not-for-profit providers. But Sweden's housing system has strong centralist features, and such a localist solution has quite simply not been considered.

A more decentralised approach would have the advantage of giving two important signals. As things are, a critique that is often made is that it is a sclerotic system that refuses to marketise sufficiently to generate rent-differentials that genuinely reflect demand. Local progress towards a genuine social rental market would clearly signal the fact that there is a continuing process of deregulation and freeing up of the rental market.

Equally important, it would provide a strong argument against asset-stripping and mass sales/conversions of not-for-profit housing, as it would make explicit its disadvantages to tenants.

The Swedish social rental market is gradually emerging, but its weaknesses are its national uniformity, and the fact that the not-for-profit housing organisations are in the form of limited liability companies majority-owned by its local authority and constituted as a subsidiary of the local authority holding company. They are therefore vulnerable to decimation as a result of - often temporary - changes in the political complexion of local government.

The government is aware of this problem and is introducing legislation to create a new organisational form - the not-for-profit organisation. This organisational form, unlike a Trust, would be allowed to make profits provided they were reinvested in the provision of housing. They would be similar to the UK's housing associations. The idea is that all local authority housing companies will take this form.

This still, however, leaves the not-for-profit housing organisation in local authority control, and as such exposed to hostile political measures.

The system in some other countries which have opted to create a mixed social rental market is instructive here. Germany and Switzerland have social rental markets but these are not only more decentralised but the not-for-profit sector is more diverse and fragmented than in Sweden, with many different kinds of ownership forms - rental co-operatives, trusts, limited-profit companies, charitable organisations and local government. This combination of decentralisation and ownership diversity makes it practically impossible for hostile local or national administrations to subject not-for-profit housing organisations to asset-stripping, and thereby to "unscramble the egg" of the social rental market.

The prospects for a free social rental market in the UK are in many ways promising. The Registered Social Landlord sector is large, and its debt burden relatively low, meaning that it should be able to exert strong market control over the for-profit rental sector if it were allowed to do so. Although the sector continues to be relatively heavily regulated by the

Housing Corporation and sometimes under the stringent control of local authorities, it is a diverse and fragmented sector (as in Germany and Switzerland) and housing associations are privately owned and managed. So the ability of a hostile government to undermine the sector is limited. By and large it can stand on its own feet. The problem with the UK is more that its for-profit rental sector is small-scale, unprofessional and poorly managed. The challenge for the UK government is to effect a shift towards a more neutral regime between the for-profit and not-for-profit rental sectors to enable them to compete effectively. Tom Startup's work offers some ideas as to how this might be brought about.

It is clearly possible for a hostile and determined government to undermine the progress to a free social rental market. It is even possible to sabotage it entirely by residualising the not-for-profit stock into a public poor housing sector, thereby creating a purely for-profit rental market. In Sweden the challenge has been local and more fragmented, but the jury is still out on whether this bold and visionary project will result in the creation of a free social rental market.